T0345893

Subjective Lives and Economic Transformations in Mongolia

ECONOMIC EXPOSURES IN ASIA

Series Editor:
Rebecca M. Empson, Department of Anthropology, UCL

Economic change in Asia often exceeds received models and expectations, leading to unexpected outcomes and experiences of rapid growth and sudden decline. This series seeks to capture this diversity. It places an emphasis on how people engage with volatility and flux as an omnipresent characteristic of life, and not necessarily as a passing phase. Shedding light on economic and political futures in the making, it also draws attention to the diverse ethical projects and strategies that flourish in such spaces of change.

The series publishes monographs and edited volumes that engage from a theoretical perspective with this new era of economic flux, exploring how current transformations come to shape and are being shaped by people in particular ways.

Subjective Lives and Economic Transformations in Mongolia

Life in the Gap

Rebecca M. Empson

First published in 2020 by
UCL Press
University College London
Gower Street
London WC1E 6BT

Available to download free: www.uclpress.co.uk

ISBN: 978-1-78735-148-6 (Hbk)
ISBN: 978-1-78735-147-9 (Pbk)
ISBN: 978-1-78735-146-2 (PDF)
ISBN: 978-1-78735-149-3 (epub)
ISBN: 978-1-78735-150-9 (mobi)
DOI: https://doi.org/10.14324/111.9781787351462

Contents

List of figures

Each of the chapters is prefaced with an image from Nomin Bold's series, depicting five Mongolian women as the guardians of the five elements (one of which is reproduced on the cover). The figures surrounding the women are dependent on them as their marionettist. All images are © Nomin Bold and are used with kind permission.

Preface

It had been three years since I was last in Mongolia, and things felt unfamiliar. The skyline was crowded by new buildings. Fashion styles had diversified. Shops and restaurants proliferated. There was also a new kind of dirty, rugged and raw side to the gloss and glamour that Mongolians are so good at upholding. As on previous visits, but perhaps more intensely simply because of the great contrasts, in 2015 I felt that I was being confronted in a somewhat dystopian way with what a capitalism of the future might look like.

Brushing up against this underside – the ruthless contrast between rich and poor, the seeming absence of the state, the horrendous air pollution in the city and the ravaging of natural resources, the unequal access to medical care and the way in which people were trying to make a living on the edges of things – provided a glimpse of the reverberating effects of late capitalism being felt in numerous places. Deeply destructive, uneven and desperate, it also appeared thrilling and full of potential. Cutting across this landscape of raw inequalities were individual people forging their own ethical projects that sometimes, somewhat surprisingly, seemed to flourish and grow in the cracks. Rather than a simple before and after (boom and bust, utopian and dystopian) narrative, I hope that through our attention to the lives of individuals will bring out a more complex and nuanced understanding of this time will emerge.

In retrospect, it feels easy to write about these kinds of experiences as the outcome of neoliberal policy and forms of austerity, about the discontent and short-sightedness of extractive capitalism with its focus on growth and greed. It is hard to make variegated and local stories count. One way in which I have been able to anchor my reflections in the changes I have observed in Mongolia is to focus on the different kinds of personal interventions into what seems so pervasive and predetermined. Elevating the stories of people that seem to go against the grain of what we may assume to be prevalent and dominant also becomes a political act of writing those worlds into being. In the following chapters I amplify the diversity that exists in spite of the shared sense that we are hurtling towards something anticipated and known. This is to deliberately side-step pervasive narratives of anthropogenic and economic crisis and focus instead on how we live in spite of such chaos.

*

In subsequent visits I became privy to the way in which my close female friends were reflecting and interpreting the economic, moral and political challenges they were facing. In contrast to the political rhetoric of men and the businesspeople I had worked with, many women seemed to work hard to create a space in which life could be tended to in another way. Alongside the violently fluctuating economy of the past few years, which had left some with nothing and others with more than they would ever need, these women were steering their way along a different path, which allowed them to reconsider moral, political and ethical choices about the kind of world they wanted to inhabit and the future this would mean for Mongolia as a nation.

The five women who are core to this book are all from different socio-economic backgrounds. I explore the kinds of lives they have been forging in the wake of recent economic growth and its rapid decline and the increasing questioning of belief in democracy. What this has opened up for many is perhaps not surprise at the fact that promises have not materialised (they do not bank on the fleeting promises of politicians), but a space in which to question past dreams and reconsider new ways of imagining the future. Innovative, creative and highly reflective, their views should be amplified above the dominant voices of squabbling politicians who rotate business and political alliances, trading in accusations of corruption.

To highlight this kind of heterogeneity is to draw attention to the ways in which wider shifts and processes are being experienced and made. Global shifts – such as neoliberal strategies of managing finance and changing forms of sovereignty and governance – do not simply create homogeneity the world over. They are shaped through individual and local projects that come to critique them, creating forms of experimentation and change. It is clear that to understand these features we need a richer characterisation of capitalist markets and the businesses within them (see Jacobs and Mazzucato 2016, 18) to look at what the economy is, beyond ideas about exchange and formal neoclassical ideas of maximising individuals.

For me, this diversity has become an important point to highlight because it is all too easy to resort to simple explanations for the way things are. That one political, economic and legal system can encompass all diversity. That democracy, as promised to Mongolia by the many international development agencies and banks, would provide a better system of governance than what was before. That developing an extractive mineral-based economy would be the way to catapult Mongolia out of debt and poverty. Such frameworks often become the descriptive explanations for activities taking place in diverse settings, both within anthropological descriptions and elsewhere. They are what Englund and Leach (2000) have referred to as an overarching 'meta-narrative' that comes to dominate much anthropology. Thus, poverty and marginalisation are explained as an outcome of neoliberal austerity practices; the rise in sovereign and personal debt is attributed to fluctuations in global commodity super-cycles; environmental and economic precarity owes to the structural inequalities of capitalism; 'subjects', it seems, can be understood to 'suffer' in the same way everywhere (Robbins 2013). Homogeneous explanations are brought to bear on diverse ethnographic settings.

The danger of explaining ethnographic diversity in homogeneous terms is what Gibson-Graham (2014), using Geertz's term, has called the danger of using 'thin description'. They argue instead that a commitment to 'thick description' may resist the gravitational pull towards forms of explanation that assume overarching, unidirectional theories of global change. Paying attention to ethnographic heterogeneity within wider global shifts becomes a way to challenge the idea that we know what these shifts are. Indeed, one might wish here to show how this very diversity comes to work recursively, determining the global shifts that we thought were familiar in the first place.

A case in point might be the way in which the mortgage market in Mongolia is being determined. Rebekah Plueckhahn (2020) asks whether forms of financialisation – such as private mortgages – create homogeneous outcomes, or whether in fact they open up different responses and experiences. Unlike in the UK and the US, Mongolian mortgages cannot attract investment from multinational foreign companies and are part of a closed network of financial institutions within Mongolia that buy debt back and forth between each other. One of the only ways this system is sustainable is through mobilising the interest earned on the mortgages being issued to the public. Strategies among banks, construction companies and apartment buyers also help support the system in diverse and incremental ways, giving rise to new strategies and economic imaginaries that proliferate out of these fluctuating, nascent networks.

Here we have a clear example where things may at first look similar (there is a rise in mortgage markets globally), but if we pay attention to the management of lending and mortgage debt we see that it is being sustained very differently in this particular context. To highlight this kind of heterogeneity is to draw attention to the ways in which economic models (or forms of financialisation) don't manifest in the same way on the ground. They are being implemented and sustained differently, owing to the local or national conditions that shape them.

Bringing ethnographic diversity to bear on wider global shifts or trends raises questions about scale and the measurement of social change more generally. Specifically, I want to draw attention here to the fact that the measurement by which one might assume global shifts are occurring might not adhere to national boundaries or use gross domestic product (GDP) figures as the unit of analysis. With massive changes in forms of sovereign power, it is clear that the boundaries of what holds things in place, or equally allows their fluidity and movement, are now increasingly determined by relationships and forms of power other than the old idea of 'the nation'. International trade networks, debt relations, even forms of pollution, viruses and waste, all cut across physical and political sovereign boundaries to determine global flows of knowledge, ideas and information.

These flows are often highly unregulated but come to determine the world we live in. They are also extremely unequal, persistently creating winners and losers and maintaining forms of environmental and economic inequality around the world. Trying to trace such flows across territories and scales is often disorientating, leaving us with a sense that things cannot be fully known or anticipated. This lack of clarity leads to speculation as to how things are, in fact, connected or determined – a kind of political second-guessing at motives and drives. In attending to these forms of speculation as they are made by our interlocutors, we may attend to the decisions and ethical projects that are undertaken within such rhetoric and to the types of explanations and connections that these give rise to. Put simply, economic and social shifts and changes may not always consist of the things we think of. They may, in fact, resist exact specification. Through attending to the ways in which our interlocutors engage with and come to know them, we may reveal connections and possibilities that we have yet to notice.

Recognising such connections presents a challenge. How should anthropologists navigate these scales and forms of explanation? Is the role of anthropology to document and show connections across scales of analysis? When doing so, whose narrative becomes dominant and when should they be amplified? In thinking through such questions, it seems to me that how we choose to pitch our explanations and the connections we choose to make is always an inherently political act that brings certain worlds into focus over others.

Almost 20 years ago, when I carried out fieldwork with a nomadic herding family on the Mongolian–Russian border for my PhD, Mongolia had a fascination with the idea of democracy and was shedding its socialist past. Today, the idea of democracy has lost its shiny newness. Shaped by an international interest in extracting minerals to fuel China's economic growth, International Monetary Fund (IMF) loans and World Bank restructuring, the last 10–15 years have seen dramatic changes in economic and political life, some of which I've tried to trace in the five-year European Research Council (ERC)-funded project, 'Emerging Subjects of the New Economy in Mongolia (2014–19)', of which this book is a part.

The project's title, 'Emerging Subjects', has focused our research in two senses. Firstly, we used this term to explore the broader themes, or *subjects*, that are emerging in the current economic climate and their articulation through different kinds of activities, from forms of political protest and stalled infrastructure projects to ways of transacting and accessing goods and cash, such as through pawnshops and barter. Secondly, we used the term 'Emerging Subjects' to refer to actual people, or to distinct forms of *subjectivity* that are being articulated as an outcome of particular kinds of economic and political experiences. These include forms of political protest, such as hunger strikes and self-immolation, and ways of sustaining life while constantly being in debt.

The group comprised 10 researchers, five of whom were based at University College London (UCL) and five at the National University of Mongolia (NUM). We were also fortunate to have a very active and diverse advisory board based in Mongolia, ranging from herders to female activists, independent economists and environmental lawyers, with whom we consulted and collaborated. While each of the 10 researchers carried out fieldwork in their own distinct areas – focusing on the property market and forms of ownership; the development of certain kinds of infrastructure; environmental and civil society movements; mining and the monetary sector; and small-scale trade in free-trade zones and in local markets – we all explored ways in which the economy was being shaped by and shaped its subjects in particular ways. We even carried out fieldwork with our paired researchers on specific topics (see, for example, Plueckhahn and Dulam 2018) and all together – when we travelled to the Southern Gobi, to Mongolia's largest copper and coal mines and to the Chinese border – along two different roads – to meet with those who transport the resources outside the country. Mongolian artists were sent our findings – in an innovative art–anthropology exchange – and responded in an exhibition in London and in our book (Spriggs 2018).

The balance between leading this project and carrying out my own research was initially alleviated by the fact that I decided to base my research on friends – the five different women central to the chapters of this book. But a more persistent problem was that the rapid change that we were all experiencing felt incredibly difficult to document. Every time we tried to do so, things shifted and we needed to revise our assumptions.

At the ERC interview in Brussels when I was applying for the grant, at the other end of the table was a woman who nodded and smiled as I spoke. Her presence emboldened me to speak up to those who posed impossible questions, and it felt like she was willing me along. A few years later I looked up her name and met Professor Hanne Petersen, Professor of Legal Cultures at the University of Copenhagen. I invited her to visit our research group, and one grey January morning Hanne sat down with us at UCL for over two hours, listening and offering suggestions and insights. We had all done some fieldwork by then and felt intensely the experience of being in a Mongolia that felt like a place we had never experienced before. What did this mean for our project? What could we contribute through our insights? Hanne embraced everything and showed us how our experiences were part of wider social and political change happening globally. When we asked her how we could write about this sense of fragmentation and change, she replied, 'Like Montesquieu; through small vignettes and essays that mimic the experiences you describe.'[1] Listening to her response, I again felt emboldened and decided to experiment with her suggestion, this time in my writing style.

Methodologically, the structure of this book has tried to mimic some of these experiences. In my writing I want to draw the reader into a particular tension that comes from living in a world where one is constantly being pulled in two directions: on the one hand, being exposed to disjointed and fragmented information about the world through titbits of information shared between friends and through social media: on the other hand, the embedded and close experience of the daily unfurling of the political and economic environment in which one lives. This tension, not unlike the space between boom and bust that I come to explore in this book, requires a zooming in and out of focus and scales of analysis.

One of the ways in which I have attempted to do this is to interdigitate each conventional chapter with what I refer to as an 'ethnographic interlude' – a snapshot or image of a particular event as it was experienced or understood, without further explanation. Looking back, I found my field notes were full of such anecdotes and exposure to unresolved events. They are experiments in taking note of things that happen at the margins of our perception (see Tsing [2015, 206] on unexpected concurrences), disrupting orderly narratives and explanations.

In contrast, the chapters themselves begin as portraits of individuals based on long-term friendship. They are ethnographically dense and replete with specifics, but while you're reading them I want you to imagine a world where nothing can be taken for granted. Progress is not to be relied upon, nor is it desired. In documenting this tension and flux I hope to show that this is not something to be feared. All kinds of creativity and innovation can be found in these spaces. From these portraits, each chapter expands outwards to explore broader structural themes that are approached and shaped by individuals.

Contrasting these two modes of writing is a deliberate act of trying to mimic the situation I am describing, where things zoom in and out of focus momentarily and then disappear from view. I hope that by amplifying this in my writing I give you a sense of what it is like to live in a world where things around you change, sometimes incredibly rapidly and without explanation, while at other times they appear, sometimes disappointingly and sometimes reassuringly, to always remain the same. In this tension we may glimpse what it means to live a life in precarity, but also how individual subjects forge a sense of community and ethical care[2] for each other as they facilitate their lives in change.

Notes

1. I took her comment to refer to Montesquieu's *The Spirit of Laws* (first published in 1748), which argues that each human society differs from every other and must be considered from all points of view. Despite being an empiricist, he 'principally stressed the fruit of observation [and] his scattered notes on a wide variety of topics, are detailed, vivid and penetrating' (Berlin 2013, 137). Furthermore, 'his vignettes of characters and situations are not stylised, neither caricatures nor idealisations', and he believed that there is no single set of values suitable for all people everywhere, no single solution to social or political problems in all countries (Berlin 2013, 143).
2. I am aware that there is a large body of literature on ethics (for example, Laidlaw 2002) and self-care in anthropology, with which I have not fully engaged. In the following chapters, I draw my main theoretical inspiration from Robbins (2013) and Zigon (2014), each of whom may be seen as part of and critiquing that wider body of work.

Acknowledgements

This book spans the 'Emerging Subjects' research project (ERC-2013-CoG, 615785, Emerging Subjects) based at UCL and NUM, from 2014 to 2019. I am very grateful to these institutions for hosting us and to the ERC for their generous funding, through which we were able to build a research community that has become an extended family over the past five years. This project began at a time when I was experiencing my own crisis of sorts as my personal life took an unexpected turn and I was forced to re-imagine the future in light of the present, just as my interlocutors were doing but on a different scale. Working on this topic with the people mentioned below has been a wonderful gift and hugely transformational in many different ways.

My heartfelt thanks and gratitude to our wonderful group at UCL – Lauren Bonilla, Joseph Bristley, Bumochir Dulam, Baasanjav Dune, Liz Fox, Rebekah Plueckhahn, Hermione Spriggs and Hedwig Waters. Together, we developed and discussed many of the ideas presented here, in reading groups, on shared fieldwork with Chiara Goia, at writing retreats and Lunar New Year parties and through our exhibitions, workshops and public talks. At NUM, I thank Sarantsetseg Dugersuren, Officer of the International Relations Department, and Boldgiv Bazartseren, Taylor Family Chaired Professor of Ecology at the Department of Biology of the School of Arts and Sciences, for facilitating our partnership, and offer my sincere thanks to our brilliant paired researchers – Tsetsegjargal Tseden, Byambabaatar Ichinkhorloo, Bayartsetseg Terbish, Munkh-Erdene Gantulga, Tuya Shagdar and Narantuya Chuluunbat – with whom we collaborated in fieldwork and research and from whom we learnt enormously. Thank you also to our fantastic research assistants, transcribers and translators – Erdenezaya Batbayar, Batdelger Doljinsuren, Batdavaa Bachaa, Setsen Altan-Ochir, Nomindari Shagdarsuren, Navchaa Tumurbaatar and Khishigsuren Yadamsuren – who skilfully assisted with recorded interviews, at conferences and workshops, in navigating formal meetings and in our writing. Our two exhibitions, conceived and developed by the immensely creative Hermione Spriggs, brought me into contact with some extraordinary

Mongolian artists and scholars, among whom I personally thank Tuguldur Yondonjamts, Nomin Bold, Baatarzorig Batjargal, Dolgor Ser Od and Marc Schmitz, Yuri Pattison, Deborah Tchoudjinoff, Uranchimeg Tsultem and Unurmaa Janchiv. I thank Nomin Bold for granting permission to reproduce her images in this book. Having a Mongolian female artist depict five Mongolian women as the custodians of the five elements of Mongolia is a fortuitous gift. I also thank our visiting (and later permanent) scholars – Marissa Smith, Sanchir Jargalsaikhan and Badruun Gardi – and our generous advisory board members – Haltar Batsuuri, Dashdemberel Ganbold, Jargalsaikhan Dambadarjaa, Badruun Gardi, Shurkhuu Dorj, Delgermaa Tsend and Manduul Nyamandeleg – for sharing their expansive knowledge and unique perspectives, as well as our Mongolian language teacher, Uranchimeg Ujeed, and affiliated member, Dalaibuyan Byambajav. Administrative assistance at UCL was generously given by Paul Carter-Bowman, Suzanne Pertou and Pascale Searle. Collaborating in research with this group of people has been a unique gift, both personally and intellectually.

In Mongolia I thank my friends for warmly welcoming me back into their lives and for all their support and critical engagement, including Lkhamsuren guai, Mandukhai egch, Bataa akh, Tserendondog hai, Dagmidmaa egch, Buyant egch, Burmaa egch, Duyaa egch, Delgermaa egch, Boloroo and their families. It is with great sadness that I record that Elbegdorjiin Eldev-Ochir, my Mongolian father, passed away during this work. I am forever grateful to him for gracefully gifting me a position as his daughter and thereby placing me in a wonderful extended family.

I am grateful too for ongoing intellectual engagement from Caroline Humphrey, David Sneath, Manduhai Buyandelgeryn, Morten Pedersen, Andrei Marin, Christopher Atwood, Daniel Murphey, Gisa Weszkalnys, Laura Bear, Madeleine Reeves, Kimberly Chong, Haidy Geismar and all the scholars at the 'Rethinking Usufruct' workshop at UCL and the 'Mongolian-Made Capitalism' conference at NUM. They have provided intellectual critique at crucial stages, and our two publications from these events (with *Central Asian Survey* and *Current Anthropology*) opened up theoretical avenues explored in this book. At UCL, I thank our head of department, Susanne Kuechler, and the Social Anthropology subsection for facilitating my research project, and the undergraduate and master's students of the 'Anthropology of Capitalisms' course (2018 and 2019) for their review of several ideas presented here. An early draft of Chapter 1 was presented at the Department of Anthropology at the University of Copenhagen, whose members I thank for their comments and suggestions, particularly Henrik Erdman Vigh. Versions of Chapters 1, 2 and 5 were presented at the Laboratoire d'Anthropologie des Mondes

Contemporains, Université Libre de Bruxelles, where I thank, among others, Olivia Angé. Hedwig Waters read Chapter 5, Bumochir Dulam read Chapter 4, Liz Fox read Chapter 3, and Rebekah Plueckhahn and Sanchir Jargalsaikhan kindly commented on the Introduction. Nomindari Shagdarsuren and Sanchir Jargalsaikhan, two exemplary scholars, did a careful job checking the Mongolian transcription. I thank them all for their insights and suggestions. The two initial reviewers and the final reviewer offered extremely thoughtful and sage advice at a time when I needed a fresh perspective. I thank them for their intellectually generous reviews. The production of this book has been blessed with several sharp eyes and editors. I thank Denise Cowle for her initial proofreading and Anthony Nanson for his thorough and astute copy-editing, as well as Jaimee Biggins, Managing Editor at UCL Press, and Robert Davies for his proofreading. Chris Penfold, Commissioning Editor at UCL Press, has seen the whole project through from its early inception. I thank him for his patience and foresight.

In London the Village Women's Co-working Group at the South Kilburn Granville Centre provided a unique space for me to write during the final stretch of this book. I am deeply grateful to My Kieri, Tom Sessink and Helena Reeves for looking after my children during research and writing. Freya and Otto came to Mongolia with me and made our research together so much fun. My has been with us during the writing of this book and has become a good friend. My immense love and heartfelt thanks to Brett Dee for gifting his steadfast support, important critique and golden stretches of time to think and write during weekends and afternoons, as well as for his photographic collaboration on *Five Heads*.

I dedicate this book to my maternal grandmother, Ebba Ekman Mannerfelt, who passed away at the age of 101 years while I was in the final stages of writing and who followed my life in Mongolia with great interest. Your absence is a gap that motivates us anew.

Note on transliteration

In this book I use the following transliteration system for Mongolian Cyrillic, as outlined in Empson (2011, xiii):

О as O
Ө as Ö
У as U
Ү as Ü
Ё as Yo
Э as E
Е as Ye
Ы as Y
Я as Ya
Х as H
И and Й as I
ь and ъ as '
Ю as Yu/ Yü (depending on conjunction with front/back vowel)

For the plural of some Mongolian words used frequently, I use the Roman 's', rather than the Mongolian plural, e.g. 'lombards'. Use of 'kh' rather than 'h' has been preserved in personal names and well-known terms, such as Khaan and Saikhanbileg. Most personal and place names have been changed, except those in quotations and those of the country and its capital city. My main interlocutors all chose their own pseudonyms.

Introduction

This book explores the lives of people who have lived through a tumultuous period of economic flux. A few years ago they were promised a particular reality if they followed certain kinds of behaviour during an economic 'boom' but, in spite of their conforming, this reality failed to materialise. Instead, the boom was followed by a period described as a 'crisis'. Rather than this leading to dissolution and disappointment, in the space between an *anticipated future* and *the unfolding present* we can discern innovative adaptations and creative openings, leading to entirely different subjects than those imagined.

Attending to this space, I mobilise a term used by one of the women who features in this book. She referred to this space as a 'gap'. Seeing this space as a gap requires a certain theoretical commitment that allows us to apprehend things from a different angle. Rather than viewing people as subjected to policies and forms of financialisation that are replicated the world over, I want to attend to the way that such encounters also allow different and variegated responses and openings; how the gap between predicted outcomes and those realised provides a space for revelation and clarity in a world that sometimes moves too quickly for us to fully comprehend.

In order to do this, I draw on many years of fieldwork in Mongolia, but specifically that between 2014 and 2019. This was a time when Mongolia revelled in being the fastest-growing economy of the world and foreigners flocked to the country to 'reveal' vast fields of minerals that 'blessed' the country with concealed rivers of gold, copper, coal and oil. Firmly embraced by a liberal democracy that allowed the sale of mining licences to explore these resources and promised its people rewards, forms of finance proliferated that encouraged national and individual spending and consumption.

By 2015, however, these promises were beginning to crack. At the time of writing, in 2019, the country and most of its people are heavily in debt. An IMF bailout is in place, aiming to implement an 'ambitious structural reform agenda, which will help to sustain growth over the medium term, promote diversification and competitiveness, and mitigate the boom–bust cycle' (Yan 2017).[1] Although the economy is in a stronger position overall than in 2015, the benefits of this recovery have not been widely felt.[2] The past few years have been both dramatic and disorientating. People have felt the fits and starts of living in response to a changing economy. Untethered from the normal order of things, the physical, social and economic environment in which people live has been destabilised and redrawn, stalled and left behind in various ways. But in this space people can also now begin to see the contours of a different terrain. This is a landscape that has begun to give rise to the articulation of nuanced critique and a desire for something different. The environment has also begun to 'act back' in the form of climate change and its effects. Attending here, we find new values and worlds being brought into being.

*

Returning to a place that I thought I knew, I felt somewhat paralysed when I visited Mongolia in 2014, because so much looked unfamiliar. New buildings, skyscrapers, businesses and outlooks shaped the skylines of people's ambitions and projects, while grievances and discontent bubbled under the surface. Things appeared to change so quickly that it was difficult to know what, if anything, remained the same. In those early days of my fieldwork for this book there was some solace, some sense of 'putting on familiar clothing', when I began to speak Mongolian again and was able to connect directly with close friends from before. Juggling the different demands of managing a larger project and my own field-work, I resorted to support from these old friends and their families. What allowed me to 'break in', to find that kernel of familiarity within the new, was reconnecting with them, some of whom I had known for more than 20 years. The idea of making them the centre of this book, therefore, came to me as an outcome of particular fieldwork constraints and conditions. It was through being with them, seeing the changes in their lives and talking with them about their experiences over the last few years, that I was able to gain a better picture of the ups and downs I had heard and read so much about in the international media. Through them I also learnt how people come to live through economic predictions and adapt them to present realities; how dreams of the future come to be transformed as different futures surface in their wake.

While making these individuals the centre of this book arose, in part, out of the structural conditions of fieldwork, it has also become an analytical choice. As I reconnected with them I found that the five women who feature in this book had shaped themselves and had been shaped as subjects in very particular ways. They come from different socio-economic backgrounds and have been held in place by wider structural inequalities and historical precedents. They have been exposed to and sought out specific events that have shaped who they are. Attending to these differences allows unique ethnographic insight into experiences of economic change. They are, among many other things, a herder, an environmental activist, a mineworker, a kindergarten teacher and a real-estate agent. It is my hope that, through focus on these individuals, different kinds of subjecthood come to the fore, providing an analytical window upon the way in which people both shape and are shaped by the economy and the historical and political circumstances in which they live.[3] I am incredibly honoured that they agreed to be part of my writing and I want to put them at the centre of this book; but first I need to give an overview of the environment in which they have found themselves over the past 10 years.

The 'bubbling economy'

Mongolians have a wonderful phrase to describe the economic conditions they have lived through. They refer to it as the 'bubbling economy' (*ediin zasgiin höösrölt*) – an economy that rises up and down very quickly and is not stable. Although they use the English term 'booming' (*büümiin üyed*) to refer to the period of economic acceleration, they don't have the equivalent term for 'bust', instead using the Mongolian term for 'crisis' (*hyamral*) to talk about its aftermath (i.e. 'economic crisis' – *ediin zasgiin hyamral*).

In the following I give a brief overview of this period and highlight some of the bigger changes that took place (more details are given in individual chapters). I then explain why seeing things in terms of these larger political and economic changes and noticing the rise and fall of GDP doesn't actually give us a very good picture of the way this period was experienced, perceived and lived through.

In the past 10 years Mongolia has felt the dramatic fits and starts of sitting at the edge of China's booming steel and technology industries, which rely on coal and copper, respectively. In 2011 it was heralded the world's fastest-growing economy, with an impressive 17.5 per cent GDP growth, owing to the discovery of vast mineral reserves, including coal, copper and gold, which fuelled the engine of its resource-hungry neighbour. With over 10 years of post-socialist shock therapy, widespread economic liberalisation and privatisation of land, property and services, the Mongolian government opened its doors to foreign investors, took out sovereign debt bonds and deregulated land laws. Its economy seemed to be skyrocketing.[4]

So enthralled was the government by the promise of economic growth that it 'blessed' its people with several rounds of lavish cash handouts based on sovereign debts that were guaranteed against future growth (see Bonilla 2014; Yeung and Howes 2015).[5] The number of banks and non-bank financial institutions, as well as pawnshops and loan companies, grew until they were prevalent on every street corner and in every countryside district centre.

Hummers became just one of several new kinds of four-by-fours that dominated the roads. Malls and high-end fashion and cosmetic shops appeared throughout the capital. Soft loans for individuals, businesses and the nation itself were easy to come by. There was a flourishing mining and construction sector, as well as the start of many small and medium-sized businesses and secondary industries. From 2009 to 2014 the economy grew by 70 per cent. In 2012 alone Mongolia attracted foreign-capital inflows equivalent to 54 per cent of its GDP (*The Economist* 2012).

In this climate, foreign mining specialists flocked to the country to purchase easily available exploration licences and 'discovered' underground fields of gold, copper, coal and oil. Spirits were high among Mongolians, the global mining community and investment speculators alike. At this 'boom time' (*böömiin üyed*), Mongolia, or 'Minegolia' as it has been called, felt like the centre of the world. Forms of financialisation developed elsewhere were quickly introduced. Mortgage schemes allowed people to buy into the growing real-estate market, relaxed licensing laws allowed people to purchase small-scale licences for mines, and different kinds of trade blossomed as new border posts to China were opened. Many Mongolians who had been studying or working abroad returned to their homeland (*nutag*) to 'look for luck' (*azaa üz'ye*) in the so-called 'Wolf Economy'.

The Mongolian government, then led by a young and dynamic Democratic Party spearheaded by two long-term friends, Saikhanbileg and Bayartsogt, implemented rapid neoliberal reforms. These played with novel models of public–private ownership and allowed new kinds of deals to be made.[6] Assets of the largest copper and gold mine in the country, Oyu Tolgoi, were split between Rio Tinto and the Mongolian government in what was thought to be a landmark deal, highlighting a novel assemblage of territory, sovereignty and rights to access.[7] In 2009 a law was passed to protect the headwaters of rivers and sacred mountains from mineral extraction; a Strategic Entities law (2007) ensured the state retained a large proportion of mineral wealth for itself. Foreign economic advisers and legal experts were not simply describing this context but were actively participating in producing it (Mitchell 2005, 298).

By 2014 the wider global commodity cycle had begun to slow down. Critique from those outside the country began to mount: Mongolians were not acting 'fast enough' on mining deals; they were exhibiting signs of being 'resource nationalists'; questioning what was happening was 'slowing things down'; and laws to protect the environment from pollution associated with mining, especially sacred mountains and the headwaters of rivers, was 'stalling development'.[8] The laws implemented to facilitate growth have become a point of critique, of policy that banked on future growth rather than stable investment.[9] Plans to build a railway to transport minerals, especially coal from Mongolia to China, were budgeted for, but the railway line was never laid. In their place, more sovereign debt bonds had to be floated on international stock exchanges to raise yet more funds to allow more deals and development. By questioning things, it was perceived – and often propagated in international media – that Mongolia would 'miss the boat'. It was just to be accepted that, in the short term, foreign companies could grab resources and land and expel local people, businesses and animals from their habitats (Sassen 2014). The success of this period was measured by its GDP, and the curve of that was starting to fall.

As inflation began to skyrocket, loans became harder to come by and businesses began to slow down. Investors began to withdraw and many disappeared altogether. Truckloads of coal were being stockpiled at the Chinese border. By 2015 most of the foreign miners had gone elsewhere (apart from a handful of men who had married Mongolian women and decided to wait things out). In their wake was a pockmarked and polluted landscape and a national economy and local population in severe debt, chained to forms of finance that had encouraged risk-taking and the promise of future growth. Outstanding loan repayments, defaulting bonds, bankrupt businesses and deserted mines (with well-paid guards to make sure they weren't pillaged by artisanal miners) littered the country, while GDP fell to 2 per cent.

Meanwhile new skyscrapers stood outwardly poised and shining, but many were, in fact, empty and deserted. Construction work slowed down, with much of it carried out through barter, so that, rather than cash, concrete was given in exchange for other materials required for building apartment blocks, materials and apartments were exchanged for Jeeps, and so on (Plueckhahn 2020). Banks were not as willing to issue loans to individuals, state salaries were not regular and funds within banks to issue loans were decreased. Many people used informal networks or the thousands of pawnshops (*lombard*) to access 'ready cash' (*belen möngö*). With interest rates of up to 8 or 9 per cent, the currency was suffering huge inflation.[10]

As global prices for coal and copper continued to decline, the Mongolian government was left standing without any security and scrabbling for ways to repay its massive public debts, apparently required by 2017.[11] Exploited by the Chinese debt market (with a 15 billion yuan swap agreement when banks were about to crash in 2015) and with fleeing foreign investors, Mongolia was testament to the fact that predicted economic growth based on high GDP does not mean very much.

By 2016 the Democrats who had brought in many of the rapid reforms were ousted and the Mongolian People's Party was elected.[12] Many of the politicians from the 'boom time' were found to have offshore bank accounts with millions of dollars hidden away for their own use and were under investigation for corruption. Disillusioned with narratives of progress, politics itself became entirely disconnected from policy and was dominated by factions of politicians who held office and sold their positions in return for payouts. Mongolians began to reflect that from the Gobi Desert, on the country's southern border with China, up to Ulaanbaatar, its capital, the country had become an empty container, pillaged of its wealth. Once again relegated to the periphery – and cast as just another story of what could have been, had they actually taken the risks the investors wanted them to, rather than retaining some sense of national authority – Mongolians were tasked with trying to put themselves and their country back together. This, quite literally, was a period they came to describe as a 'crisis'. As the economist Batsuuri has commented:

> Given falling GDP, an increasing budget deficit, decreasing foreign reserves and other negative macroeconomic indicators, experts agree that Mongolia is in economic recession, if not in crisis.
>
> …
>
> The combination of high public debt and rapid private-debt growth means that an imminent economic crisis in Mongolia is now fast approaching. (Batsuuri 2015, 3, 10)[13]

While public debt was a large shadow looming over the government, private debt was also ubiquitous. People speculated that over 80 per cent of retirees were in debt, their pensions being a major source of collateral against which to take out loans for family members. Taking loans from those who had already taken out loans was also prolific across the private and business sector, leading to multiple chains of indebtedness.[14]

In this context of flux and change, people were caught between accumulating debt and engaging in illegal activities to pay it off. The government sought the support of the IMF for a bailout package to avoid defaulting on its bond obligations, which was agreed in 2017.[15] This set in place austerity measures that would see some stabilising of the economy.[16] At the same time, Battulga, one of Mongolia's more renowned and wealthy businessmen and a wrestling champion, was elected as president. Appealing to many as a more down-to-earth 'populist' leader, he has implemented some more authoritarian changes during his leadership. In April 2019, for example, he fired the country's top judges and the head of the anti-corruption agency. In August of the same year he met President Trump in America.

Discontent with democracy and the rise of populist nationalism

On a graph documenting GDP per capita the period of fieldwork on which this book is based would appear as a jagged line. In summarising events I feel the need to give dates, at least years, so that one can get a sense of the rapidity of change. On reflection, however, I realise that this kind of summary tells us very little about what it was like to live through these shifts. It doesn't tell us about the way people felt about, engaged with and understood the economy, both as a practical day-to-day experience and as a way of understanding wider political and economic changes. Instead we might ask: what does living under such conditions make people think of the idea of democracy, of capitalism as an economic system, and its commitment to progress?

One immediate outcome of living through these fluctuations is that many Mongolians have become increasingly critical of the idea that democracy, as a system of governance, can bring about progress, as propagated by the international donor and financial agencies that have flooded the country for more than 20 years. Since the 1990s, when Mongolia first committed to the idea of democracy, many felt it was just a matter of time before Mongolians 'caught up' with the foreign countries whose political system they had now joined, allowing them to follow a linear step-by-step path towards development. Given the dramatic stops and starts over the last few years, however, many now reflect that progress through democracy is not a straight line. Instead they see that the path winds, drops away and falls out of view, only to re-emerge again in an instant, then to be lost for something else. Many still want 'development' (*högjil*), but not through democracy, which is considered a corrupt, broken, chaotic and extractive system with sharp climbs and sudden falls, riddled with inequality and competition. In many ways neoliberal policies have been conflated in people's perception with ideas about democracy, to its wider detriment, as merely part of capitalism and productive of widespread corruption among elites. Many lament that perhaps democracy is not the right path for Mongolia at all (see Chapters 2 and 5). And it's no wonder – the last few years have been full of contradictions, indeterminacy and precarity.

It is out of such concerns that many question the wisdom of having 'followed the yellow heads' (i.e. Euro-Americans), generating what some have labelled more 'populist nationalist' forms of critique. Along with such discontent, protests against the government and its decisions have increased. People are bored of hearing politicians talk about 'foreign direct investment', 'freedom' and 'the market' – terms that have dominated political speeches for some time. They are also disillusioned with the promise of economic growth associated with large-scale mining and foreign investment. There is a growing sense of disconnect between people and the business and political elites who do not appear to listen to concerns that are being raised. Many of the more critical voices, for example, have been silenced, with the imprisonment of environmental activists and the dismissal of a labour unionist who set himself on fire during a press conference to highlight the plight of mine workers losing their jobs to a Chinese company takeover. Such views are often associated with ways of seeing and imagining the future which threaten the power of the ruling elites, and they are dismissed as 'nationalist' or 'populist'.[17]

For example, Ganbaatar, an independent MP labelled 'populist' by the ruling elites but voted the top politician nationwide by the public in 2015, gave an interview on the TV chat show *Talk with Me* in October 2015, voicing such concerns:

> Multinational companies [are] stealing and digging our wealth, without benefiting my people. International institutions – IMF/World Bank, Jeffrey Sachs [sic], are always feeding this, asking for privatisation. Only 13 families have benefited from this ... there must be something wrong with neoliberalism.[18]

He went on to explain how Mongolians are only able to survive in such uncertain times because 'Mongolian nomadic life and tradition teaches you the ability to respond and adapt' (*Nüüdelchin am'dral bolon Mongolyn ulamjlal n' hümüüst olon züiliig surgaj baidag*). While many complain about wealth accumulating among the few, they also elaborate how Mongolians are good at adapting to experiences of rapid change precisely because of their nomadic heritage, a somewhat essentialising perspective that, nonetheless, generates a feeling of pride in the ability to survive even the most difficult of conditions, such as 'wild capitalism' (*zerleg kapitalizm*).

Many feel that the elites have kept what wealth there was for themselves and have 'mixed business with politics' (colloquially referred to as 'to layer your coat' – *davhar deel*) to such an extent that this is what politics is these days. Levels of corruption and deceit fuel the view that the people in power cannot 'carry' (*barih*) the nation. Bribery (*heel hahuul'*), corruption (*avliga*) and factions (*frakts*) characterise politics, which has come to be determined by what some refer to as the 'invisible side of the economy'. In this world, no one is simply a herder, a businessman or a trader. Everyone, my friend explained, is at least two or more things. Learning how to juggle and manage this multiplicity is how people survive.[19]

*

Below I explore the way that the term 'crisis' both opened up a space for reflection and shaped the imaginative potential in the gap. For now, let me say that, although critique of Mongolian politicians is widespread and considered acceptable, in general there is a very intense performative imperative that presses hard on people on a day-to-day basis to speak their worlds into being – to literally act out the world they want; something that scales outwards from the individual, the family, the district or homeland one comes from, to the way people talk about the nation itself. This is both a cultural belief (that critique can be damaging) and a politically performative strategy to keep others at bay. It is a way to resist possible encroachment of one's national borders (by China or Russia), given the very real fear of being eclipsed by such encroachment. The imperative is felt so keenly that even in the now ubiquitous situation where everyone is somehow dependent on economic activity of some sort with China, one has to uphold the idea that Mongolia is a nation functioning almost completely independently, albeit with some third-neighbour relations, such as America, Japan or Germany.

National pride plays an important part. It often influenced how people wanted to present things to me as a researcher. Sometimes it would come to my attention that people were acutely aware of not talking too badly about the context Mongolia had found itself in, not least because, they reflected, my writings could influence future foreign investors and business leaders. In this vein, critique of politicians and their policies is often blamed on non-Mongolians and becomes a rejection of democracy as a colonial project that enables corruption and wealth accumulation among the few, most of whom are not considered 'pure' Mongolians.

In many ways, the theoretical concepts of 'performativity' and the individual practice of 'prefiguration' – terms that will become important in the following chapters when I illuminate a gap between an ideal or hoped-for future and its current manifestation – are but iterations of the same idea of 'bringing worlds into being'. One emphasises technical restructuring and abstract prediction and can involve non-human algorithms and metrics. The other is born out of a political idea that it is the personal choice of individuals to act the world they want to into being. Both draw on speech act or performative theory (see Austin 1975; Butler 1988) and are based on a commitment that change – through language, individual action or non-human technical networks – is possible. However, they differ radically in the way they understand that this change can occur.

For example, in his study of economic financiers, Holmes (2009), following a more actor–network theory approach, argues that economic markets are the artefacts of language and the technical means to control them. Following Callon (2008) and MacKenzie and colleagues (2008), such an approach takes the view that economists do not simply 'observe' markets but affect them by saying what they are doing, should do and will do. A case in point is the way in which foreign direct investors, as well as financial speculators, attempted to determine the pace of economic change in Mongolia, through recourse to language that threatened a 'resource curse', 'resource nationalism' and the impending 'slowing down of the economy'.

Prefigurative politics, on the other hand, points to a more individual-orientated modus for transformation (rather than a systematic one determined by algorithms). Graeber states:

> prefigurative politics means making one's means as far as possible identical with one's ends, creating social relations and decision-making processes that at least approximate those that might exist in the kind of society we'd like to bring about. … [it is] the defiant insistence on acting as if one is already free. (Graeber 2014, 85)

Both projects attempt to shape the future according to present imaginings of what is right or desired, and in that sense they mimic the power of prophecy, signalling that narratives about the future very often tell us more about what is valued and desired in the present than they do about how that future will unfold (see Empson 2006).

As mentioned above, Mongolian language etiquette almost always contains an element of prefiguration and performativity. 'Talking the world into being' is a widespread vernacular Buddhist belief. The performative nature of language is well recognised through the idea of 'black and white speech' (*har/tsagaan hel am*),[20] where a kind of defiant utopianism is adhered to in order that it will affect the world around one. A well-structured exchange is almost always followed when greeting someone one hasn't met for some time. A predictable set of responses is almost always given when asking about the state of someone's family or herds, and a question about health is almost always followed by an immediate response that the responder is fine. This happens across scales – as much among financiers and businesspeople as among national politicians, individuals and friends. It is not that people are confined to an always-positive view of the world, even when things are unequal, insecure or unjust, but that on the surface, at least, a way of describing the world that one is living in is important because it is held to define it. After polite exchange, and if relations of intimacy and trust are deemed appropriate, more details may be divulged and a fuller description is revealed, but even then, to dwell on negative aspects is to invite them to determine the future. This is why 'black speech' (*har hel am*), or talking badly about someone/something, is viewed as a potential curse that can bring the world spoken about into being.

Sometimes this narrative exchange and the outcomes it is hoped to engender falter and a gap begins to take shape between the two. During the period I am describing, people commented that things were happening so quickly that they often 'seemed unimaginable just four years ago'. The gap, as one of my friends put it, between the future that was imagined in 2011, when GDP was so high, and the one that was currently being realised was one where dreams and wishes had to be revised and new futures imagined. In the following I use this ethnographically derived concept of 'the gap' to think through what happens when futures – through economic prediction, government policies or, simply, individual dreams and aspirations (the kind of prefigurative politics described above) – are lived and realised as something completely different from how they were initially imagined. I ask what kind of opening is created in this space and how it is accommodated into future imaginings, for both individuals and the nation.

The gap

In her conversations with me my friend Oyunaa often reflected on the past few years as a time of becoming accustomed to living in 'the gap'. This was a space located in between a binary: between an anticipated future and the reality of that future as it has now materialised. In the course of my fieldwork this gap was only just becoming perceptible as a specific period of time and no single moment had been allocated to it (in spite of Mongolians liking to divide up time into periods with specific names). To take this term as a starting point is to isolate and define a space of expectation-now-thwarted and an attempt to describe what is in its place. It is to marshal an ethnographic concept as a theoretical tool to open up a space that might otherwise pass our attention.

However, I am keen to stress that this was not simply a place of thwarted dreams and disenchantment, a narrative all too familiar among ideas about neoliberalism (or dark anthropology, à la Ortner [2016]). Instead, inspired by my interlocutors, I have chosen to focus on the way in which people forge new paths in this space – a practice that also allows them to revaluate past beliefs and ideas. Taking this approach is both an ethnographic fact and a deliberately political act. Attending to the way the five women who are core to this book forge a life in spite of thwarted predictions allows me to highlight the creative ways in which people make a life through exposure to forms of financialisation that leave them in debt and networks of corruption that seem to work against them at every turn. It is to show how people work hard to 'prefigure' a future they want (i.e. deliberately try to live a life they would like to come into being), as part of individual ethical projects. This is to suggest not that people are free to simply choose the futures they want, but that 'optimism', as Lauren Berlant has commented, is 'a scene of negotiated sustenance that makes life bearable [even] as it presents itself ambivalently, unevenly, [and] incoherently' (Berlant 2011, 14).

Amplifying optimism in a context that could be viewed as exploitative and desperate is important because, as Robbins (2013) has highlighted, we need to pay attention to the fact that people who appear to be suffering in different ways must also imagine better ways to live, and we need to hear them. The better worlds they imagine and their ways of trying to get to them surely differ in significant ways, and it is important for us to learn from these differences so that we may let their efforts inform our own (Robbins 2013, 459). This is a provocation to push us out of easy homogenising forms of explanation that see people subjected in similar ways to forms of inequality the world over. It is to heed Tsing's call to attend to the 'acts of noticing' (Tsing 2015, 37).

In attending to these acts of noticing we can begin to see how the gap can act as both an *ethnographic* and a *theoretical* marker. As a conceptual space it is somewhat familiar to other spheres. In economic anthropology, for instance, substantivist anthropologists noted a 'gap' between formal economic models and their substantive realisation on the ground, in markets, industry and finance. Anthropologists continue to draw attention to this kind of slippage when they focus, for example, on the way in which financial institutions are upheld, enacted and realised through particular social interactions that are not in themselves part of the models the financial institutions seek to sustain. Of course, not all economic behaviour is structured by existing cultural norms, nor does self-interest drive all economic behaviour, but this does not detract from the very real work that goes into people's ongoing work in making economic life liveable. We know that '[c]apitalist economies are not theoretical abstracts but complex and dynamic systems embedded in specific societies' (Jacobs and Mazzucato 2016, 17), that 'orthodox economic theory which underpins most current policy-making does not provide a proper understanding of how modern capitalism works, and therefore how to make it work better' (Jacobs and Mazzucato 2016, 12) and that, '[c]ontrary to the claims of orthodox economists that "the laws of economics are like the laws of engineering: one set of laws works everywhere", there are in fact many different kinds of market behavior, and several varieties of capitalism' (Jacobs and Mazzucato 2016, 19). In political anthropology, this slippage, or gap, is sometimes referred to as 'vernacularisation'. Here, vernacularisation occurs between political (sometimes state) visions and their local articulations and realisations.

In the anthropology of the subject, the inter-subjective moment is often highlighted as a slippage, fallacy or 'gap'. So 'recognition is the misrecognition you can bear, a transaction that affirms you without, again, necessarily feeling good or being accurate' (Berlant 2011, 26). Here the gap points to a misrecognition or sense of paradox that you notice but hold in place in your relationship with another (not unlike the underlying sense of misrecognition felt from basing policies on future economic predictions). For example, even though 20 years have passed since I first met many of the people who feature in this book, I am still humbled, surprised and bewildered in my relations with them and recognise that any account I give contains a gap that is very much my own. In the anthropology of kinship, like the substantivists, anthropologists questioned the use of Western models to study other societies. A little more than simply cultural relativism, they asked if there was in fact a gap, or slippage, between the conceptual terms they were using to understand the phenomena they were observing (the term 'sister', for instance, did not always refer to the same set of relations everywhere – i.e. biological ones). Attending to these gaps, not simply as aberrations, we can see how – if we suspend our own conceptual categories – the world can be made and remade differently.

Ethnographically, in Mongolia this gap opened when belief in economic growth began to change from hopeful anticipation to mistrust and doubt as people began to challenge a vision of the future propagated by international investors and shotgun policies (see Borup et al. 2006; Graeber 2012). To use Graeber's (2012) phrase, the 'paradox of performativity' exposed the gap between the future imagined and the future as it was being experienced, as a retroactive logic began to erase past visions and the present seemed like the only logical outcome. At the same time that people began to discern the cracks between the 'vision' and the 'reality', a new kind of subject was beginning to emerge and shape the economy from the ground up. Attention to the kinds of subjects emerging in the gap is, therefore, a way to attend to the slippage between the future imagined and the future realised; between a new way of seeing oneself in the world and that which was propagated before. Here the Mongolian term *zai* – meaning space, gap, interval or distance between two points – may not be entirely fitting. The term *zöröö* – meaning discord, variance, disagreement or difference, such as a difference between a dream and reality – may be better suited.

Theoretically, it is important to think through this ethnographic instance of discord, variance, disagreement and difference. By elevating it we can open up a space that allows us to think back on what the economy is and what kinds of subjects it has engendered. It allows us to question the limits of the use of our term 'the economy' and what it obfuscates as a theoretical category in our analysis. This is what Wagner (2018) has referred to as the 'reciprocity of perspectives', whereby a particular moment allows a simultaneous looking back and forward at the same time. Here the gap is a space that is neither the past (the ground) nor the future (the figure, exemplar), but the line in between the two. In the following chapters we will see this space in between two things: between a model of economic growth based on mineral extraction and the consumption of fossil fuels, and the lived reality of implementing that projection (Chapter 1); between democratic revolutionary ideals and the lived reality of corruption, crony capitalism and sovereign debt bonds that that system allows (Chapter 2); between the idea that microfinance and small-scale loans alleviate poverty, and the networks that have to be cultivated and cared for in order that people are not drowned by debt (Chapter 3); between policies that engender forms of ownership and practices of temporary possession (Chapter 5); and between individual agency and freedom and the collectivities that hold one in place (Chapter 4).

Attending to this space – to the line that joins the past and future together (or an anticipated future and a felt reality) – allows a degree of reflection, a shift of perspectives, of movement and speculation. Indeed it was under just such circumstances that the past few years have been thrown into relief, becoming perceptible for people in a way they hadn't quite been able to grasp before. This is what Wagner calls

> [c]hiasmatic time, [a time that] makes use of the self-contradiction inherent in the double proportional comparison to coordinate two contravening and antipathetic 'kinds of time': the recollective *past in its own future*, and the anticipatory *future in its own past*. The former makes sense of a past event from the perspective of its own consequences in the present day, whereas the latter means we can only predict or forecast future events on the basis of evidence available in the here and now. (Wagner 2018, 508)

While I see the gap as a space straddling binaries, it is not an endless deferral as in a Deleuzian type of void: things crystallise and take hold here. While the gap allows a kind of folding of the past into the present, it is a revised and updated version of that past, owing to current experiences. In Mongolian, people refer to this revision and adaptability of one model or vision into another as a basic feature of modern life. To *mongolchloh* – to 'make Mongolian' – means to adapt to things as they appear and are given (often from 'outside'), and to revise one's plans and activities according to those changes, so that within a knowable yearly cycle difference is incorporated and accommodated. Within formal narratives of performativity and prefiguration or 'the white speech of everyday life', the world unfolds unevenly and at a different pace. Attending to these kinds of values, which are articulated and practised by my interlocutors, I follow Robbins's (2013) call to move away from a focus on the so-called 'suffering subject' – as well as other focuses that stress 'resilience' in late industrial capitalism – and explore instead what *futures* people themselves imagine and what *lives* or, to use Jarrett Zigon's (2014) phrase, *worlds* are being lived. We need to think recursively – through the reciprocity of perspectives that anthropology allows – about how those lives may come to inform our own.

Crisis and the gap: openings and possibilities

In this context it is important to ask why the term 'crisis' (*hyamral*) was used to describe what was going on and what work it came to play in shaping ideas about what was happening. In her book *Anti-Crisis*, Roitman highlights that though 'crisis is an omnipresent sign in almost all forms of narrative today' we need to explore what work the term 'crisis' plays 'in the construction of narrative forms' (Roitman 2014, 3). Labelling something as a 'crisis', she shows, draws attention to it as a specific event and highlights it as an irregularity or rupture. Often, moments of crisis are defined as events 'when normativity is laid bare', when partial knowledge claims are disputed, critiqued or disclosed (Roitman 2014, 3–4). Here, use of the term 'crisis' creates an opening that allows one to rethink what counts as the norm.

In many ways, in Mongolia the term 'crisis' was deployed to signal an opening or rupture like that described by Roitman (2014). For many, this was a 'bursting moment' (*höös hagaralt*) that showed that the economy was going too fast: things could not keep up with the models as they were being implemented. It allowed people to recalibrate, to take stock and to re-establish things. Many spoke about the crisis as 'good for Mongolia because it would mean more realistic goals for the future'. Like Oyunaa's idea of the gap, 'crisis [was] a blind spot that enable[d] the production of knowledge' (Roitman 2014, 39). For Oyunaa and Zedlen (Chapters 1 and 4, respectively), for example, rapid economic change punctuated by 'crisis' allowed them to re-evaluate what and who they wanted to be and how they might be able to live in this environment.

Roitman further highlights that 'crisis is not [always] a condition to be observed ... it is an observation that produces meaning' (Roitman 2014, 39). Here we see the performative aspect of crisis as a point of observation, giving a reading of a situation in its own image, so to speak. Trapped within its own conceptual parameters we can only have crisis or anti-crisis (Roitman 2014, 92). Similarly, the term 'economic crisis' was used by the media and foreign observers in this performative sense to signal failure. It was a way of punctuating time, opening up a necessary space for wider commentary and critique, most notably of the state and of politicians, and for a discussion of what proper sociality and transactions should be like. Instead of taking capitalism for granted – as an already determining structure, logic and trajectory – through such narratives a continually questioning atmosphere has become the norm. This echoes Povinelli's idea (2011), developed in *Economies of Abandonment*, of a space 'between *potential* and *actual* alternative social projects'. It points to the spaces and communities that exist in a precarious world of *potential existence* without ever actually changing completely. Here the idea of 'crisis' aligns much more with the idea of the 'gap', where a space opens up providing conditions for new forms of sociality.

To attend to this idea of crisis as a productive space is to move away from the idea of epochal or event-like thinking (à la Roitman 2014), and instead to enquire into what is taking place here and now, reminiscently perhaps of Tsing's description of 'living in capitalist ruins'. In the following chapters we see that these 'heterogeneous spaces provide the conditions for new forms of sociality and for new kinds of markets and market instruments (or "products")' to be employed (Povinelli 2011, 17). To highlight the birth of new forms of sociality born through such spaces, making them the focus rather than the deviation, is to provide 'a much better understanding of how modern capitalism works' (Jacobs and Mazzucato 2016, 2). In this light it is important to note that the term 'crisis' was almost always paired with the term 'economy' (*ediin zasag*), loosely meaning the governance of property, highlighting the interconnection of politics and the economy.[21] This broader interconnectedness was reflected in the way people commented that 'the economic crisis is happening all over the world isn't it, not just in Mongolia'. Here we see a sense that, while local politicians were to blame, the economy was also something outside the nation's control: it fluctuated globally, regardless of state intervention.[22]

In its ubiquitousness, recourse to 'crisis' can indeed become durational. Vigh (2008) argues that we need to see crisis as a new kind of 'context' – a terrain of action and meaning rather than an aberration. Here, uncertainty, precarity and indeed recall to 'crisis' are ongoing features of late capitalism that evacuates the 'near future' (à la Guyer 2007). A sense of things hanging on a fine thread has in many spheres become the 'new ordinary' (see Berlant 2011). There is, it sometimes seems, no *not*-crisis.

When crisis becomes a terrain of meaning rather than a moment or aberration, then it holds a certain 'cruel optimism', to use Berlant's (2011) phrase. Here crisis becomes the regular and ordinary. In many ways it signals the way that we have become normalised to forms of disorder. Berlant argues that the term 'cruel optimism' refers to a 'condition of maintaining an attachment to a significantly problematic object' (Berlant 2011, 24) such as a fantasy or future life that can never be reached, in this case the idea of economic growth, continued consumption or a world outside financial and environmental crisis. Berlant (2011) explores how this fantasy has less and less relation to how people actually live, or can ever live. How do people adjust between life and fantasy and the spreading anxiety about what is happening, has happened and will potentially happen next? They do so, she argues, by continually maintaining a kernel of optimism – something that makes life bearable, even as it presents itself ambivalently, unevenly and incoherently.[23] Optimism is a way for people to adjust to the loss of a fantasy of the good life, to crisis as the ordinary.

There is a sense in which the gap and the adjustment (or reciprocity of perspectives) that takes place there are exactly those which Berlant's subjects engage in through holding on to a sense of optimism. Within this kind of 'new ordinary', others have also highlighted the flourishing of optimism, hope and difference in such spaces (see Miyazaki 2006; Pedersen 2012, Zigon 2014). A sense of hope, we will see, becomes a pervasive way to control the uncertain, often through an attention to managing the personal. Saruul, my 'Ulaanbaatar grandmother', with whom I always stayed while in the city, maintained this sense of control and optimism by memorising all the code endings of food items that were made in Mongolia versus those that had been imported from Korea or China. She kept these numbers at the forefront of her mind every time she went shopping and urged me to do the same. Managing what she ate and knowing where it came from gave her a sense of control. It was an optimistic way of making life bearable, and when I was in that world it felt completely coherent. Crisis could be kept at bay. We need to articulate ethnographically the way people manage the emotional contours of life during such precarious times.

Economic diversity and hope

Roelvink, St Martin and Gibson-Graham (2015) have argued that to focus only on what has become hegemonic – such as shared forms of subordination, inequality and corruption – would be to simply reproduce knowledge about the way the economy performs and makes itself into being, leaving us impoverished of the diverse economic imagination and performances outside this. In a similar vein the work of Tsing (2015) and Bear and colleagues (2015) also emphasises that we should not take the idea of capitalism for granted. Although neoliberal economic policies were implemented to create capitalist realities maybe the same the world over (loans, mortgages, etc.), these forms of financialisation are taken up and experienced differently, being based on contingent networks that are constantly changing. Importantly, the 'diverse economies' approach calls out the sin of 'capitalocentrism' (a hegemonic view of capitalism) and argues that to talk of 'alternatives to' capitalism is to represent the economy as essentially singular, rendering invisible the non-capitalist economies that exist in the shadow of capitalist relations.

To take this approach is to acknowledge that capitalism is not simply experienced differently in different places (a kind of substantive relativism), but that it is also *made differently* by subjects who are determined by the historical experiences they are exposed to. Following these calls to attend to diversity within, Tsing argues that '[i]t is time to reimbue our understanding of the economy with arts of noticing' (Tsing 2015, 132). It is important to take time to notice the diversity that exists within known structural frameworks, because it is often such diverse non-capitalist elements (those things without capitalist value) that exist on the edges on which capitalism depends (Tsing 2015, 66). This is marshalled in Tsing's idea of 'salvage economies', where she looks at the role of natural resources as the drivers of monetary economies (see Chapter 5). To attend to the formation of these natural, as well as emotional and spiritual, 'resources' is to notice 'the divergent, layered and conjoined projects that make up worlds' (Tsing 2015, 22). Rather than focus on the figure (the known monolith that is capitalism), one can focus on the ground from which it emerges. Rather than explore the model, one can see where it is located, how it is shaped and handled, who shapes it and under what circumstances. Rather than survey supermarket stock lists to see what people are purchasing, one may attend to the purchase of food types through code endings enacted by someone like Lhamsuren to control her fear of degenerate consumption and its deregulation.

This is to claim not that economic models do not exist and act upon the world, but that there is always slippage between the model and the reality (see Mitchell [2005] on the work of economics). It is very much this slippage between (1) an economic model and its reality, (2) political theory and its realisation in practised democracy, and (3) an essentialised idea of Mongolia as a nation, and the reality of what its people are doing, that focusing on the gap illuminates. If we take seriously the idea of attending to this space, not as a momentary or liminal phenomenon, but as something that may be the ground on which we have to dwell for some time, then we must acknowledge that economic activities do not always unfurl in a progressive way: that what takes shape here may become the norm, that, ultimately, it may become the background for its own figure that shifts the foundations of what we think of as the economy. Paying attention to and recognising this is, then, a political act of amplification; of attending to those things that often go unnoticed and are unrecorded. It is to draw attention to the space between that which has been promised and hoped for and that which actually materialises. It is to make visible a new version of what is.

The point to stress here is that there is not only ruination (Navaro-Yashin 2009) when structural models (both physical and analytical) fail to materialise. Productive and positive outcomes are also born out of such failure. Certainly, many have concluded that mining does not lead to the progressive developmental stepping stones promised by international donors and investors. Banking on a single economy has generated more precarious livelihoods and less security. Instead of relegating this to the periphery, as something that does not fit a neat timeline of progress, or to a reality that has failed to live up to a model, we can bring this 'loss of traction' in from the edges of our observation and allow it to rest in the centre.[24] This makes the gap the foreground rather than a line that joins two time periods together (before, boom / after, bust). It recognises new conceptual ground and highlights alternative routes that shape people's lives.[25]

This investment in documenting divergent life projects sidesteps an analysis that takes a totalising (and often predetermined) framework, something that ends up reproducing itself across the world (see Bear et al. 2015). In the following chapters we see how women like Sara, Tuyaa and Delgermaa (Chapters 2, 3, and 5) are committed to forging ahead in spite of various structural obstacles that hinder economic profit. Their innovative approaches are driven by a kind of ethical commitment that life continues in spite of uncertainty. This is an attempt not to dwell on iterations of 'individual micro-freedoms' (Petrović-Šteger 2019) at the expense of broader structural injustices, but to highlight a 'vernacular timescape' that attempts to 'wedge' (Nielsen 2014) itself in a landscape of 'crisis ordinary' (Berlant 2011) and co-create new kinds of present (see Petrović-Šteger 2019).[26] The term 'vernacular timescape' helps us to shift our focus from the (re)production of broader structural inequalities and the reproduction of crisis and precarity, and attend to some of the individual ethical projects of world-building that are taking place in this space (see Zigon 2014).

Through attention to the intimate ethnographic lives of the following five women we see how life in the gap opens up new ways of thinking about the future, sometimes subverting senses of anxiety into clarity and hope, giving vigour and energy to everyday life projects. Here the gap has worked productively to open up a temporal framework in which people are increasingly critical of ideas of democracy, giving rise to a revaluation of what counts as moral and ethical leadership (see Chapter 2). This prefigures, as Sara does, a future that one wants to come into being through one's religious practices. Instead of being pulled down by conditions of precarity and uncertainty, Tuyaa (Chapter 3) constantly calculates new ways to secure the care and welfare of those around her, through a process I have come to describe as a kind of 'ethical calculus'. Her choice to move away from familiar networks into a world that is insecure does not just mean an unhinging from things. It provides new opportunities and relations for her and her family. In Chapter 4 we learn of Zedlen, who is a state worker for the Department for the Environment, posted to the north-easternmost countryside province to manage water reserves – a job no one really wants – but who nevertheless embraces the challenges and difficulties of her position with energy and ingenuity. Zedlen describes herself as a singularity, a hangover from a previous generation, amid a society that has radically changed its values and priorities. However, it is precisely this new society that has allowed her to exercise this way of being – giving her the space to advocate and fight for the values she believes in. Her ability to sustain this position in a broader world of flux owes as much to her own individual work as to the world that allows her to execute that work. She is, in many ways, an exemplar of the context she critiques; it frees her from the chains and networks of remaining in place.

Highlighting the very distinctive ways my five interlocutors engage with time to allow new openings and possibilities makes visible the varied perceptions of what is. This looks beyond the idea that the last 10 years were a fleeting liminal phase that existed 'out of the ordinary' (as boom/bust, before/after, crisis/non-crisis). It focuses instead on the way in which this period has become an enduring present and one that is increasingly bearable and even optimistic; a place where lives are lived and made, and different futures are imagined, even for the same person, so that new alternatives can be carved out within the existing present. It makes the gap the foreground, rather than relegating it to a temporary (or liminal) line that joins two time periods together, and recognises that it is a space for the emergence of new kinds of subjects.

Subjects-in-the-making

I hope that you have begun to get a sense of the diversity of subjects that flourish in this space. Here I deliberately want to use the term 'subjects' in a double sense. On the one hand, I want to draw attention to the kinds of topics – themes and concerns – that arose in the gap. On the other hand, and this is what I want to turn to now, I also want to highlight the kinds of subjectivity or actual subjects that are made in and through such processes.

In doing so it is useful to remind ourselves of what Foucault referred to as the 'three modes of objectification which transform human beings into subjects' (Foucault 1982, 777). One of these modes is the way human beings turn themselves into a subject, and the other two are what he refers to as objectifications through language, or through the pursuit of wealth and in economies, or through dividing practices (such as existing institutions). Through these modes, Foucault elaborates,

> There are two meanings of the word 'subject': subject to someone else by control and dependence; and tied to his own identity by a conscious self-knowledge. Both meanings suggest a form of power which subjugates and makes subject to. (Foucault 1982, 781)

It is important to draw attention to the duality of the term 'subject' (i.e. subjugating and making subject to). Through this we can see how people both are the authors of their own subjectivity (open to create and choose who they want to be) and are subjected to wider forms of power, as well as cultural norms and historical trends and expectations that shape them (Faucault 1982). Ethnographic and philosophical insights have shown that these can be processes that are folded in time and history, with a subject that is in a continual process of becoming and emerging (à la Deleuze 2006), or they can be distinctly singular and defined by events that shape people in individual ways (Humphrey 2008). Out of such singularity, people can also be isolated as types or figures who come to dominate the cultural landscape as modes or ways of being (see Humphrey 1997), standing for general types of people (Lindquist 2015). Like exemplars (Humphrey 1997), they emerge in processes of rapid economic flux and political dissolution and transform into figures whom people aspire to be like or revere.

In thinking about these processes, I have found it helpful to draw on the work of three scholars who address very different ideas about subject formation. The first explores the impact of historical/biographical determinism (Garcia 2010). The second attends to singular events (or decision-events) as shaping subjects (Humphrey 2008). The third explores ideas about figures and types as exemplary for future forms of subjectivity and comparison (Lindquist 2015; Humphrey 1997). These three different theoretical positions of subjectivity are necessary because, on the one hand, people living in Mongolia have been subjected to forms of political and economic transformation and exploitation for millennia, more recently during the Manchu and Socialist periods and, since the 1990s, with neoliberal democracy. My subjects are deeply entrenched in different kinds of historical determinism that shape who they could and can become. However, although I aim to analyse how individual lives have been affected by these larger historical and political processes, I also recognise their unique singularity as they confront and shape the processes to which they are exposed.

This is perhaps why I think that debates about the structural legacy of post-socialism actually serve to limit rather than to deepen the analytical work we can do here. Academics of post-socialism often argue that current economic and social forms in Mongolia are but iterations of those found in other post-socialist countries. Their similarity can be accounted for because of pre-existing socialist ways of doing things – through networks, favours and factions – that existed before the 1990s but are now inflected with new pressures, demands and forms of uncertainty (see Ledeneva 1998). Although certain kinds of relationships and ways of doing things may continue, I would argue that this kind of analysis paints over a complexity with a kind of historical determinism. In part this is because the term 'post-socialism' is often used in a catch-all sense to refer to a series of 'socialist ways of doing things' whereas there was in fact a 'proliferation of various kinds of socialisms and alternative futures generated from socialist experiences around the world' (Channell-Justice 2019). Moreover, as forms of financialisation have proliferated since the collapse of the Soviet Union, debt has become a major feature of individual lives and of Mongolia as a nation. People are indebted to banks and institutions (as well as to each other). The Mongolian nation is indebted to its neighbours, through monetary swap agreements, or to companies through abstract bonds, meaning that the idea of the sovereign is not held in place in the way it was before. Not only is money loaned on a national level, but other kinds of resources including minerals are given on loan to leverage payments and future securities (consider 'The Chalco Affair'). All this means that the workings of 'the economy' and 'the state' are not simply defined by 'post-socialist logics and experiences'; they are inherently modern, current and fluid. As Thelen (2011) has pointed out, the idea that there was a simple transfer of economic concepts from one era to another impedes nuanced analysis, reducing it to a branch of area studies. In contrast, she argues, 'despite the embeddedness of socialism in global processes, new theoretical horizons will emerge only if we take Otherness seriously and move beyond normative analysis derived from economic perspectives' (Thelen 2011, 54), particularly those which deemed socialist economies to be inferior to Western ones. Mongolia is, in many ways, unique in the post-socialist world in that, although it sits between two socialist monoliths, it has managed to mobilise democratic capitalist reforms in quite rapid and new ways. What we see in the following chapters is not so much the remains of socialist ways of thinking *in relation to* global processes but a familiarity, as well as difference, that is structured by the specifics of current conditions and experiences, something that both opens up and forecloses certain kinds of activity and forms of subjectivity.

Angela Garcia (2010) has similarly straddled this analytical balance between the influence of the past and the newness of the present (but on a different scale) in her study of dispossession and addiction in New Mexico. She explores how personal history is interwoven with cultural and political history. Though foregrounding the inseparability of personal experiences from history and the broader world, she stresses, to a degree, the singularity of the subject (Garcia 2010, 2).[27] In many ways this is a classical Deleuzian view of the subject as endlessly coming into being, or becoming (Deleuze 2006). It pays attention to the way in which a subject both is made through the historical and structural conditions in which they live and also flourishes independently.

Anthropology has often prioritised approaches to personhood that stress the way individuals are relational subjects situated within wider historical networks. Here the subject is always defined by and through its relation with others.[28] Several of the women I focus on can be said to exist in the midst of their relations with others, being situated in networks and historical conditions that hold them in place.

In contrast, Humphrey (2008), following Badiou, has highlighted the way in which individual subjects are shaped through very particular events (which happen to them or which they choose). This is a way to conceptualise singular analytical subjects that burst away from the past (and historical determinism) and are constituted in particular circumstances, bringing about a rupture of previous knowledge. This intentional subject is very much in contrast to the idea of the subject shaped in historical time and in relation to others. It is shaped by particular 'decision-events' when multiple strands of personhood achieve a kind of unity and singularity (see Chapters 2 and 4). Humphrey (2008) enquires how we can account for intentional individuals when so much of anthropology highlights the interconnected nature of social relations and subjects, and proposes that 'individuality as an actable-on capacity may be attained through decision: the "plumping for" a specific way of being a person, if only temporarily, and by prioritising the keeping at hand of divergent multiplicities in an emotionally cogent, internally shuffle-able array of possibilities' (Humphrey 2008, 363). Decision-events, then, may be seen as occasions when the multiple strands of personhood achieve a certain unity and singularity. Finally, and taking my lead from Lindquist (2015), I am also interested in the way in which kinds of subjectivity, either processual or singular, become a template for a kind of exemplar, embodying particular ideals that people choose to live by (see Chapters 2 and 3). Here a study of the subject becomes an anthropological entry point that illuminates broader contexts and processes from particular positions, allowing a comparative ethnography of capitalism to emerge.

As contrasting theories of subjectivity, these three approaches can help us to understand the processes that shape people. Rather than each subject being defined by a singular process or mode, I find that processes that we might define as ones of individuality and commensality are evident in each subject.[29] One way to think through this coexistence of past and present is to apply Deleuze's concept of subjectification created by the 'fold'; of the exteriority folding into one's interiority and back again (O'Sullivan 2010). In this layering and folding, the subject (both the person and the wider topic illuminated) is made in different ways, reciprocally, both determining outwards and being determined by and drawing from the outside. People as much as the economy, we will see, both shape and are shaped by the conditions in which they exist.

Thus it is important to note that the women whose portraits are drawn in this book may not recognise themselves in the chapters about them. I have interpreted their narratives and experiences against the wider 'vistas of history and the scale of global patterns' (Bear 2015, ix), building creatively from their experiences to think in broader terms beyond the individual to trends and changes, in a reciprocity of perspectives. Their stories are starting points, or triggers, that allow us into lives and to 'notice the divergent, layered and conjoined projects that make up worlds' (Tsing 2015, 22). Like the women studied by Pelkmans and Umetbaeva (2018) I have 'selected, organised, connected and evaluated' biographical elements (Riessman 2005, quoted in Pelkmans and Umetbaeva 2018, 1055) to draw attention to broader subjects as they arise from the individual narratives.[30] Each of the women also has a very different way of narrating and understanding the changes she has experienced. It is in attending to these that different understandings of subject formation arise.

Part of the reason for organising my chapters by subjects, or people, rather than by themes, is that in the course of my fieldwork I found that my friends each had very different narratives about how they had come to understand what had happened to them. Since they were situated in unique positions to observe this change, I also felt that their perspectives provided interesting openings and perspectives on to wider themes, providing insight into the way people are shaped by economic experiences and forms of financialisation and how forms of financialisation and economy are shaped by people. This recognises the dialectic between the way in which individual people shape the economy and the way they are shaped by economic policy and change. Povinelli (2011) has argued somewhat similarly that 'conceptualising neoliberalism as a series of struggles across an uneven social terrain allows us to see how these heterogeneous spaces provide the conditions for new forms of sociality' (Povinelli 2011, 17).

Amid these heterogeneous spaces there was also a constant: the gendered nature of our dialogue. In the course of my travels to and from Mongolia I have developed close friendships with these five women, whom I consider in Mongolian kinship terms as my 'older sisters'. My earlier research in Mongolia, which began in my early twenties (when there was no mobile phone coverage, or any opportunity to call 'home' except by pre-ordered calls at the central postal office in Ulaanbaatar), was foundational to these friendships. These women cared for me over long periods as a 'daughter' or 'little sister' when I was distinctly 'out of place'. Over the course of our now more than 20 years of friendship I have reciprocated that care in various ways, looking after their daughters or helping when things were hard. We have witnessed many of each other's transformations and changes. They are almost all slightly older than me in age, grew up during the socialist period and experienced the dawn of democracy unfurling in their country. They have had to remake themselves in several ways over the years and have often resorted to working collaboratively and in innovative ways with their partners or other family members for subsistence.

In many ways the post-socialist and democratic context has granted Mongolian women a broader repertoire of possible subject positions than it has done men, who often (perhaps from a female perspective) seem constrained by ideas about what counts as masculinity, having to reproduce national ideals and templates.[31] Finding the time to talk privately, to catch up on events that had been happening in each other's lives and learning about the changes, was a normal part of our friendship. Such exchange signalled, perhaps, a gendered form of Mongolian intimacy between women, allowing an affinity and closeness I don't always allow to flourish in the same way in my friendships at home (see Stadlen [2018, 16] on the reluctance of women to speak in general terms and on gendered speech).

During the course of my fieldwork, there was also an element of them wanting to help me, to assist any way they could as they saw me juggling the demands of the wider research project and personal commitments, often with one or more of our children at our sides. The recounting of stories about our lives, as we stole moments of privacy in otherwise busy lives, was shaped by stylistic convention and exchange as well as the traces of individual hands (see Walter Benjamin, in Jackson 2013, 227). Sharing stories about our lives takes us both into and out of ourselves. These moments often belong to spaces of inter-subjectivity (a reciprocity of perspectives) as we journey back to where we began, but with a transformed understanding of the past from the perspective of the present (Jackson 2013, 246). The act of undergoing such inter-subjective transformation through our exchanges brought our friendships alive, turning life experiences into stories that fuelled reflections on wider things that were happening in Mongolia. Through sharing information about our individual lives, we reflected on broader themes and changes. Opening ourselves up to each other as people who faced difficult choices and deliberated over decisions, we came to reflect on things in general.

Although I have started this Introduction with a discussion of the political and economic developments in Mongolia over the last few years, this book can be read very much as a book about Mongolian women. I place them at the centre as both a stylistic and an analytical choice. Although their lives are brought into juxtaposition here as an outcome of my own movements (they do not all know each other – although some do – and it is unlikely their lives would become interwoven in the real world), placing them side by side facilitates insight across scales, economic, social and political, in a way that adherence to the idea of a 'single' fieldsite would not. In fact, there are many ways in which the singularity of place as marker for 'site' is a false concept in Mongolia. People are highly mobile (in terms of physicality of place), something facilitated through networks and extended kin, meaning that whom they live with, and where, changes frequently. Change and heterogeneity do not mean randomness or chaos. The women in the following five chapters will understand my description and recognise each other's descriptions of what is going on in Mongolia today.

Summary of chapters

To end, I give a brief overview of the core chapters. **Chapter 1** introduces Oyunaa, a woman who worked with her husband who had returned from abroad with savings to try their luck at a handful of different business ventures in the emerging Wolf Economy, only to be thwarted at different turns. Oyunaa's chapter highlights how individuals deal with moments of crisis, concealing aspects of life from some while sharing their problems with others. It illustrates the temporal fluctuations in economic life as people try to steer a course through choppy waters. In this chapter Oyunaa coins the term 'gap' and reflects on the period of rapid economic growth and decline that her people have lived through. Now employed by Mongolia's largest gold and copper mine, she finds her place first as an environmental compliance officer and then as a procurement officer in the capital, remaining the main breadwinner of her family.

Interlude I. What happened to the Tuul river? This interlude introduces the way in which politics is currently discussed in Mongolia, as rumour about the motives of politicians rather than discussion about policy. It sets the scene for why snippets of information such as this interlude are important examples of the way that information emerges and is shared. It takes the example of the drying up of the Tuul and the rumours that surrounded that, as well as the lack of interest when the actual reason for it was revealed. The interludes provide breaks in the chronology and invite the reader to notice things that unfurl on the edges, which may otherwise be obscured from view. A written manifestation of the world I am describing, they cut into the humdrum of daily life with snapshots of events as they reveal themselves. More like impressions than full descriptions, they provide a background hum of partial comprehension.

Chapter 2 draws on the life of Sara to explore emerging forms of political critique. It highlights important points about national identity, who can be trusted to 'carry the state' and what role historical exemplars play in the search for a new kind of governance. Following her interest in historically informed religious movements, we learn about a practice in which people turn inwards, attending to their souls, to gain knowledge for a new kind of subject. This is a processual kind of subject who folds the past into the present and, in so doing, works with others to prefigure a new kind of idealised future. Politically astute and part of an educated elite, Sara sits at the forefront of a new kind of political consciousness.

Interlude II. This interlude juxtaposes the description of a young man working in a sewing factory that makes bags to transport copper concentrate from Mongolia to China with an image of the men who work at the copper concentrate plant loading the bags on to trucks, along with the trucks driving along the dusty roads to the border with China.

Chapter 3 focuses on Tuyaa, who lives in the peri-urban settlements of Ulaanbaatar's ger district. She works full-time at a state nursery, where people leave their children in the morning and sometimes don't return until 10 p.m. She is a single mother and the sole carer of her blind mother. Having just got the job, she doesn't miss a day of work because she is collecting state stamps to be able to claim her pension in a few years' time. Recently she was diagnosed with a cancerous tumour and had her womb removed. She has to travel by bus to the hospital and pawn her jewellery to raise the funds for her medication. Following Tuyaa, we learn of the pressures of intergenerational care, the movement of people from the countryside to the city, the lack of state provision and the importance of family networks. Unhinged from her natal networks, she is dependent on the state, constantly trading in favours in order to keep going. Her life jumps from one kind of event and decision to another, rather than accumulating over time.

Interlude III. Chains of debt: accessing 'ready cash' through 'material loans'. This interlude provides insight into the way people access cash from pawnshops. It documents the practice from the perspective of both the pawnshop worker and the person taking the loan and highlights the chains of ownership involved in such transactions.

Chapter 4 follows Zedlen, a state worker in the Department for the Environment, posted to the north-easternmost province to manage water reserves – a job no one really wants. On the one hand, Zedlen describes her singularity and difference as a product of her generation amid a society that has radically changed its values and priorities. On the other hand, it is precisely this new society that allows her to live this way – giving her the space to advocate and fight for the values she believes in. The world she inhabits is changing rapidly, yet she holds on to certain things that she believes in and wants to remain the same. Women of this generation, like Tuyaa, appear to live in a world where the ground is shifting underneath them, without a solid place for them to dwell. But, unlike Tuyaa, Zedlen seems to thrive in such transition; it frees her from the chains and networks of remaining in place.

Interlude IV. This interlude documents the life of Baysaa, who works for an international bank during the day but channels the spirit of Attila the Hun at night, writing books as guides for new ways of living. The seamless way in which she talks about moving between these worlds highlights, among other things, the way in which capitalism is never a single entity but contains extreme diversity within it. In a similar way, in one subject we also see the multiple people she juggles to be.

In **Chapter 5** we learn of Delgermaa's various countryside businesses, funded with the help of loans from the local bank and from individuals. Through their different projects I examine the ways in which people use and convert resources in the local environment so they can enter into wider commodity supply chains to make a small profit. These businesses are sustainable only because they rely on networks in which people lend to each other through informal means.

Interlude V. This interlude documents the business ventures of an urban businessman and traces his attempts to secure wealth in property through a tale of three different projects – one hoped for, one realised and one stalled.

In each chapter the gap that emerges is something slightly different: between a vision of a future successful business and the reality that unfolds (Oyunaa); between a previous version of oneself and current political action (Sara); between migratory dreams and current realities (Tuyaa); between a learnt morality and current politics (Zedlen); and between economic models of microfinance and salvage economies (Delgermaa). Rather than stopping people from living, this dissonance facilitates a range of ways in which people have been able to remake themselves as subjects. In doing so they are critiquing ideas about democracy and the economic processes it supports – as certain things become visible that previously appeared opaque. The gap is not so much a fixed condition as an opening or rupture, out of which new ways of seeing the world are born.

People all the time work hard to create alternative worlds for themselves and their families amid the forces that try to hold them in particular ways, drawing on the 'cruel optimism' (Berlant 2011) that flourishes in spite of people's realisation of their compromised attachment to a world that attempts to hold them in a particular place. It prefigures, as Sara does, a future that they want to come into being, while they work hard to maintain relations between networks of individuals, as Tuyaa does, so that life can move forward in spite of the near total retreat of the state. Rather than see Mongolia simply as a place of thwarted dreams and disenchantment – a narrative all too familiar with ideas about neoliberalism – I have chosen, like my informants, to focus on the ways in which people forge new lives and subjectivities in spite of futures that have failed to materialise. We owe it to our interlocutors to observe, to document and to amplify this.

Notes

1. For further information see: www.imf.org/en/News/Articles/2017/10/30/pr17411-imf-reaches-staff-level agreement-on-the-first-and-second-reviews-of-mongolia-eff.
2. Gan-Ochir Doojav (Chief Economist of Mongolia), while arguing for a more 'sustainable growth model', claimed that, '[s]ince 2016, the poverty rate has fallen by only 1.2 percentage points and is still high at 27.4 %. ... very few residents are benefiting from the mining sector

and a significant amount of the revenues generated from the country's high GDP growth are paid back to non-residents' (Doojav 2019).

3. This is not to detract from their sharp individuality and singularity, also present in each of their cases.

4. In 2012 *The Economist* ran an article titled 'Booming Mongolia: Mine, All Mine', but in 2014 it published an article with the title 'Mongolia: The Pits'.

5. These handouts served to placate the population at a time when people were beginning to be nervous about the extractive economy. As a symbolic sharing of wealth they attempted to manage increasing instability and critique (see Yang 2013).

6. Mongolia tends to focus on implementing new legislation rather than resort to jurisdiction or common law to challenge things. For example, Resolution No. 27 of parliament (adopted in 2007) designated 15 mineral deposits across the country as 'Strategic Deposits' and 39 mineral deposits as potential Strategic Deposits. According to the Mineral Law (2019), the state may hold up to 50 per cent equity interest in an entity that holds a mining licence for a Strategic Deposit. (If this deposit reserve has been determined using private funds the state may hold up to 34 per cent.) Furthermore, parliament has the right to designate a mineral deposit as a Strategic Deposit (see the Mongolian Mining Law 2019 for further details). Other influential legislation includes the 1997 New Minerals Law (whereby 60 per cent of the country was ceded to mineral exploration). The 2009 law with the long name (see Chapter 4) created no-go zones for mining through the designation of sacred mountains and the headwaters of rivers.

7. The Oyu Tolgoi deposit is a Strategic Deposit jointly owned by the Mongolian government (34 per cent) and Turquoise Hill Resources (66 per cent), which is listed on the Toronto stock exchange. Rio Tinto owns 51 per cent of Turquoise Hill Resources. More than 16,000 people are employed at Oyu Tolgoi, of whom 93 per cent are Mongolian nationals. Although this is a very large project, Mongolia can't expect to see any revenues from it for at least another 15 years. Development at this mine has not only been under geopolitical stress; it is also under geological stress. Attempts to expand underground have led to collapsed tunnels, rendering sections inaccessible. Furthermore, the Mongolian government has ruled that the mine must be powered by a domestic rather than Chinese energy source, from Tavain Tolgoi powerfields, 150 km away (see Ker 2019).

8. Similarly, Appel notes, 'Resource-curse theory in Equatorial Guinea not only helped create the world it posited, but also helped create a politically consequential distance between something called the national economy, on the one hand, and local experiences of state violence and corporate power on the other' (Appel 2017, 296).

9. The largest coal mine owned by a Mongolian company stockpiles coal at the Chinese border which is continuously sold at cut prices.

10. The need to repay bank loans, especially in the construction sector, meant that people could not demand such high prices for their buildings as previously, but had to accept lower prices – or even forms of barter – to meet payments.

11. The Mongolian parliament amended certain articles of the Minerals Law of 2006 in October 2017. The amendments changed the mechanism for obtaining new exploration licences, moving to an open tendering system. These amendments also modified the procedures for applying for and granting a licence.

12. Sanchir Jargalsaikhan kindly drew my attention to the fact that, despite signing the so-called Dubai Agreement in May 2015 on the Oyu Tolgoi mine's underground expansion (http://ot.mn/media/ot/content/Agreements/2015–05-18_OTUMDAFP.pdf), which promised huge benefits, the Democratic Party was unceremoniously ousted from power. Around this time the Democratic Party had also given away exploitation rights to Tavan Tolgoi mine (from the state-owned Erdenes Tavan Tolgoi) to a consortium consisting of the Mongolian Mining Corp, China's Shenhua Energy and Japan's Sumitomo Corp (US$4 billion worth of investment in the project), a step widely critiqued as going too far and halted at the parliamentary level by their own party member and Speaker of Parliament Z. Enkhbold and future president Kh. Battulga (https://af.reuters.com/article/commoditiesNews/idAFL3N0X42ID20130401/?sp=true).

13. 'Mongolia certainly meets the criteria for a crisis' (Batsuuri 2015, 12). 'This crisis may materialise at the start of 2017, if not earlier, as the government has to repay its accumulated debts in the first quarter of that year' (Batsuuri 2015, 13).

14. Most of the private debt, Bastsuuri continues, was 'incurred during the so-called "mining boom" years of 2008–12' (Batsuuri 2015, 12).

15. In 2017 the IMF in-country representative Neil Saker commented, 'Loans issued at a low inter-est rate will improve the debt burden … The loans will improve confidence in the market. Pol-icies to strengthen the banks will lead to lower interest rates, job creation and more inclusive growth. Reduced banking risk will also stabilise the currency' (Kohn 2017). Meanwhile Khash-chuluun Chuluundorj, an economist at the National University of Mongolia, also commented in 2017, 'This is a break from the past when the government was only doing populist things, like distributing money or stocks and lowering taxes.' He highlighted further that people are demanding better governance: 'As Mongolia's foreign policy and economic apparatus expand, there seems to be a growing gap between the government and its people' (Lkhaajav 2017).
16. See: https://uk.reuters.com/article/uk-mongolia-imf-idUKKBN18L0AC.
17. One member of our advisory board pithily summarised with a Mongolian phrase the way resource-extracted wealth accumulates among those in power: 'The caravan is moving, the dogs are barking, but no one is doing anything' *(jinger nohoi hutsaj l baidag, jingiin tsuvaa yavj l baidag)*; elaborating further that 'the government is like a young man spending his father's credit card without any thought for the consequences. We need to cancel this credit card and look at the internal situation.'
18. www.youtube.com/watch?v=dsFCwkUK4xU.
19. The twists and turns of wider political and economic change are important for many people because, even if they do not affect their lives directly, these events do have traction in people's imaginaries; they use them like markers on a chart to plot routes during uncertain times (pers. comm. Sanchir Jargalsaikhan).
20. Højer notes, 'Literally speaking, *hel* can mean "tongue", "language" or "news/message", whereas *am* can mean "mouth", "words" or "speech"' (Højer 2004, 50).
21. Plueckhahn and Dulam (2018) note that the Mongolian term for economy (*ediin zasag*) con-sists of two words: *ed* meaning 'article', 'item', 'thing', 'property', 'possession' or 'wealth' and *zasag* meaning 'governance', 'rule' or 'authority'. Together they mean the 'governance of prop-erty' or 'possession authority' at the individual, household and state levels. This combination means that, as Sneath has argued, 'the very definition of the economic sphere depends upon the notion of political authority' (2002, 201), highlighting a cultural interconnection between politics and the economy.
22. Many people in their forties commented that, although uncertain and tempestuous, the con-ditions were not comparable to the early post-socialist period, when many went without ad-equate food and clothes. They often used the availability of foodstuffs in shops as a point of comparison.
23. Her work 'turns toward thinking about the ordinary as an impasse shaped by crisis in which people find themselves developing skills for adjusting to newly proliferating pressures to scramble for modes of living' (Berlant 2011, 8).
24. 'Indeed, as many progress narratives lose traction … it becomes possible to look differently', allowing us to attend to 'what has been ignored because it never fit the time line of progress' (Tsing 2015, 21–2).
25. Bear and colleagues (2015) argue along similar lines: '[i]nstead of taking capitalism a priori, as an already determined structure, logic and trajectory', they ask 'how its social relations are generated out of divergent life projects'.
26. Commenting on people's relationship to past war in Serbia, and engaging with critique by Ivan Rajković (2018), Petrović-Šteger (2019) comments, 'One of Ivan Rajković's conclusions (2018), in an excellent article describing the demoralization of Serbian factory workers, is that anthropologists are too ready to romanticize an idea of the "inner freedom" of discarded workers, rather than engaging in an analysis of the socio-political conditions that have seen them cast aside. Of course, we should beware of praising ethnographic micro-freedoms – of studying only the micro-worlds in which systemic victims or 'losers' are free to express a local resistance to power. Yet my ethnographic experiences of the last four years suggest that it can be equally wilful – equally a sop to academic populism – to be nothing but ironic about people's orientations to the future and to their expressions of hope. Many in Serbia remain possessed by the war – a typical motif of academic literature and popular culture; but equally some, as I have seen, are going to great lengths trying to co-create people's collective understanding of the present, their sense of a vernacular timescape' (Petrović-Šteger 2019, 1).
27. As an anthropologist, Garcia (2010, 2) notes, it is often hard to think and write about such singular, personal experiences.

28. Deleuze elaborates on the process of subjectification created by the 'fold; [as the process] of the exteriority into interiority' (Deleuze 1993, 77–8).
29. Maintaining this tension is what Jackson has referred to as 'one of the most difficult and urgent problems we face whenever we attempt to account for the course of any human life[.] [The problem] is how to project a sense of its singularity while also doing justice to the historical, biogenetic, genealogical and social forces that shape it' (Jackson 2013, 225).
30. This selection extends recursively to their telling of themselves to me, which could equally be seen as a form of 'ethical discourse', a way of self-curating themselves, describing the kind of subject they would like to be seen as (Jackson 2013, 29).
31. This is further reflected in the fact that women often have a wider range of employment options than men (including in the caring and administrative professions). If not involved in 'business', men often resort to temporary hard labour, illegal, semi-formal or herding activities (pers. comm., Liz Fox).

Figure 1 'Earth (soil)' *Shoroo*, by Nomin Bold, 2016. Acrylic, canvas 245 × 145 cm.

1
When the party was cancelled

What happens when you have more than 300 guests booked to attend a party and prohibition is suddenly enforced across the country? This is the situation I will explore in this chapter, when my long-term friends Oyunaa and Tüvshin decided to become Mongolia's biggest party organisers. With a team of employees they converted an old socialist warehouse into the most desirable party venue in the country. News spread and, miraculously, a few weeks before opening they had reservations for 300 guests, twice a day, for the next three months.

Two weeks into their business, however, they received an early-morning knock on the door of their apartment. Oyunaa opened the door to find several policemen standing there. The night before, there had been a serious alcohol-related car accident resulting in ten deaths. From that day on, the police explained, alcohol would be prohibited indefinitely across the country and they would have to shut down their business.

Oyunaa closed the door and sat down on the floor. All of their capital had gone into this investment. They had taken out several loans and employed a large team of people. Their apartment was filled with boxes of food and alcohol that reached the ceiling. After the initial shock began to dissipate, it dawned on her that from this day on their lives would inevitably have to take a very different course from what they had imagined. This chapter examines what they made out of this seemingly desperate situation.

It highlights how people live through failure of economic predictions on a national scale; how a change in policy, based on an accident, is experienced by individuals and enables them to revaluate multiple factors in their lives. In doing so it explores how forms of financialisation that have been developed elsewhere – in this case different kinds of bank loans for business ventures – are imported into Mongolia (see also Chapter 5 for a similar case). Often actively promoted by development agencies and foreign advisers, these systems do not simply flourish in the way intended. A major factor in this gap between the model and its actual use is the extent and stability of the wider market in which it is used. If the market is unable to sustain the level of continuous business needed to reproduce and bolster the system, gaps appear where things do not flow in the way intended.

As the anthropologist Bumochir Dulam (pers. comm.) has highlighted, there exists, for many, the counter-intuitive situation that one 'has to [engage in alternative activities, which may appear from the outside as "corrupt"] in order to appear to follow the rules'. Auditing, for example, can be carried out through the purchase of a stamp rather than through the scrutiny of accounts; 70 per cent of state pensions are used as collateral to access loans to pay off debts; and goods and services are retained within networks and groups that share and distribute financial burdens and apply for funding as one company rather than as conglomerates (see Chuluunbat and Empson 2018). Through such practices, and many more, the surface appears to function in the way intended, but underneath things are different.

This difference is mainly one of maintaining a complex web of prospective future outcomes in the face of their proposed singularity. Although political and economic rhetoric may promote singular visions to embolden people to take risks and contribute to wider state projects, a commitment to networks and their multiplicity are a major feature of Mongolian social life (Sneath 2006). Multiple projects are maintained, not so much as a result of uncertainty and marginalisation but in order to keep several futures open as possibilities. This is something that Oyunaa had to relearn after she had become disconnected from life in Mongolia through spending some years abroad.

The party organisers

I first met Oyunaa in 1998 when she was visiting a friend's flat in Ulaanbaatar. At the time she was living in the countryside with her parents. I met her again at various times in Mongolia, and then in England when she and her husband Tüvshin were working illegally at a pheasant farm, sleeping in a cold caravan in a muddy field in the Leicestershire countryside. When I came to Mongolia in 2008 I stayed in their flat. Tüvshin had just been on a trip to China to purchase cleaning equipment to sell and their apartment was full of different kinds of mops and buckets. It was a disconnected place with people pursuing multiple independent projects. The TV was constantly on, drowning out any attempts at lengthy conversation.

In 2015 we met again, this time over dinner and on trips to the countryside. Our sons played, and we began to reconnect and to learn about what had been happening in each other's life. Oyunaa told me how the flat I had stayed in had been repossessed only a year later and they had lost everything because they couldn't repay their mounting loans.[1] One Saturday morning, we found ourselves in a coffee shop on the outskirts of Ulaanbaatar with a few hours to talk. I don't have the space to recount the whole of Oyunaa's story here, but the following is a summary.

*

'At the time I thought my marriage was finished,' explained Oyunaa, somewhat out of the blue, before describing how life for her and her husband had been very strained in the UK. She had wanted to return to Mongolia. He had not. Sometimes she would walk along streets with tears streaming down her face and he would not know what to say. After almost two years in the UK they separated and she returned to Mongolia, only to find him unexpectedly waiting for her in the arrivals lounge. Reunited with their daughter, they set about building a new life for themselves.

Having made savings while in the UK, Oyunaa and Tüvshin were wealthy when they returned. Tüvshin had managed to save £8000 (16 million *tögrög* [MNT]) working in the hotel and catering business, while Oyunaa had saved £5500 (MNT11 million) working at the pheasant farm and in retail. They bought a car and a flat and invested their savings in the party-organising business.[2] This was to be a very innovative economic endeavour: it was the first independent party-organising company in Mongolia, with a 500-person-capacity party hall. They invested all their money in the business and got several loans from the bank.

> We had tables, aprons, plates, all sort of things. Just like in England when we worked for a catering firm. So we set up a proper comfortable luxury party hall. And we invested 60 million *tögrög* for that. We rented a location. We paid for it and renovated the socialist factory into a party hall. When people came to see it, they were just so excited and said, 'Let me in. I can't wait to see it.' … All the days were booked. Everybody wanted to have a space here.

From 1 December to 1 January, they had a minimum of 300 people booked twice a day.

> We worked for one month solid with no sleep, in order to clean and decorate and set everything up, and then we started our party, on 1 December. And then ... on 6 December, in the morning, somebody knocked on our door very early. There were two policemen there. They said, 'You are the biggest party organisers in Khan Uul district, and last night in Baganuur there was a serious incident related to alcohol. Ten people died so we will now prohibit all organised parties and the sale of any alcoholic drinks. We don't know how long this will continue for.'
>
> Can you imagine! How we were dreaming ... You can calculate – 300 people, two times a day means 600 people and each person has to pay MNT25,000 tax. So how many *tögrög* we could have earned in a day? For 31 days? So we were going to earn more than MNT100 million per month. What we had left on that day was MNT6 million in cash and MNT8 million in alcoholic drinks in our flat, and an MNT48 million loan in the bank. So this idea, you can imagine, it completely bankrupted us and there was no party.

Prohibition continued in Mongolia until the early spring of 2010, but at the time they had no idea how long it would last.

> We owed so many different people money – to those we had employed, to the bank, to different suppliers, to the guests. We gave all the beers and vodka back to the company (APU), but we still had lots of hard liquor which we had bought from the market, and that was about three million *tögrög* just in alcohol. So, what we did is – actually one of our employees initiated this and asked, 'Can you give me this vodka for my salary?' So we gave one million, no, two million *tögrög's* worth of vodka to our employees as their salary. That left us with one million *tögrög's* worth of vodka in our hands. Our kitchen was stacked so high with boxes of vodka, whisky, scotch, gin, liquor and things ... including a party set for 30–40 million *tögrög*.

When Oyunaa was describing this catastrophe to me it seemed unreal, but what she went on to say was equally so:

When all of this happened I was just so down – I was in shock and stayed at home, sleeping maybe 12–14 hours a day. Slowly, however, Tüvshin began to put together a plan. He went out every evening and began to sell the alcohol from his backpack. In this way, we got enough for our daily food. But I just hated to see people because it was the biggest loss in my entire life. They began knocking at our door asking to buy alcohol and I would just look at them with a shocked expression and say, 'No, what are you talking about? We don't sell alcohol here.'

Oyunaa went on to explain how she came to understand what had happened. She had imagined a future, she said, and in that future they had already reached their destination, but suddenly these dreams were shattered.

By April, they had sold off all their alcohol reserves and her husband had begun work on a simple website for tourists. They involved their family members and drew on extended networks in the countryside. Some people paid upfront for tours, and that summer the couple cooked and drove them around while their parents looked after their daughter. In December they had a son. Just when things seemed to have started to pick up, in 2011 they were unable to keep up their mortgage repayments and their flat was repossessed. Too ashamed to tell their relatives, they spent the next year living in a friend's small wooden house without winter insulation or heating, on the outskirts of Ulaanbaatar: bankrupt, unable to ever take out a bank loan again, and with the shame of their collapsed business.

The gap: is a party a reality that can be sustained?

Following this dramatic narrative (which has been considerably abridged) Oyunaa reflected on their experience in two ways. Firstly, she highlighted what she called a 'gap' between the *vision* of what they thought they could achieve and the *reality* of what had happened:

At the time, we didn't see the gap. The party business was something we wanted to copy from what we had seen in England. But we aimed too high; we didn't assess properly the legal, social and cultural factors that would determine what we could do. If we had been in Mongolia for some time, we would have been more in tune with what was realistic and possible. We aimed too high, taking out all these massive loans. It was bound to fail. Even though we are Mongolian, and had been away for less than two years, in our minds we were really far away.

The gap between a *vision* and the *reality* of putting that vision into practice is something that was described to me by many of the young and middle-aged Mongolians I met who returned from living abroad once the mining boom began. With the promise of future economic growth, many sacrificed savings and investments and put their dreams into action through innovative projects.

After two years at home, on an off-chance and prompted by her husband, who tore out a job advert from a newspaper, Oyunaa applied for a job as an environmental officer for a large mining company. Because of her background in biology (she has conducted extensive research on the Mongolian pheasant) and previous work experience in Mongolia she was offered the job and worked at the mine site for several years, spending months at a time away from her family on a fly-in/fly-out basis. Tüvshin continued to run his small business and looked after their two children. During this time they slowly got their lives on track, working and developing new projects simultaneously with relatives and extended family. They have now managed to buy a new apartment and their daughter is able to study at university. Oyunaa works at the mine's office in the capital city and dreams of one day running a small café. At last, she reflected, their expectations were in tune with their surroundings. They have transcended the gap that brought them back in the first place.

Nomadism and the wild path of capitalism

As outlined in Oyunaa's concept of the gap, when people bring innovative models from elsewhere and apply them to different contexts, the vision inherent in the models often fails to meet the reality in which it is placed. Experiencing this mismatch, Oyunaa and her husband began to wonder how their friends were able to maintain a steady pace, moving from one short-term loan to the next, not earning very much but finding – I use her term – 'a sustainable way to live'. This final point reminded me of many of the people I knew who were trying their luck at multiple business ventures, surviving from one loan to another and never saving any money in their bank accounts, in what some call a manifestation of Mongolia's 'wild capitalism' (*zerleg capitalism*). In these activities a lack of permanence permeates almost every sphere as people juggle different projects, jobs and opportunities, all the time moving from one thing to the next while maintaining multiple chains of indebtedness.

Although most people did seem to be surviving from one small loan to the next (whether from banks, non-bank financial institutions, pawnshops or friends), they were rarely able to pay off these loans through the business the loan funded. For a start, the repayment period is often too short and the interest rates too high for any business to begin to reap profits. Instead, people often resorted to some secondary business to pay off the initial loan, or relied on friends and family to bridge repayments. Somehow, juggling these different economic commitments, people do seem to maintain some level of equilibrium: children continue to go to school, fees for universities are found, new clothes are bought and cars and homes are maintained.

Substantive differences exist in the ways economic models, such as microfinance loans, are appropriated and experienced. Indeed, in the ways that such models are adapted on the ground we can see again the gap between the model of how banks or financial institutions may *perceive* that their services can support the growth of local businesses and the *reality* of how these services are actually experienced. Earlier in the autumn of 2015 the head of the United Nations Development Programme in Mongolia vividly described to me how such 'a life in debt' (to use Clara Han's 2011 phrase) must mean that the general population lives on a day-to-day basis with incredible levels of stress and anxiety. Recalling his insight, I asked Oyunaa if the endless movement between different projects and endeavours, so prevalent among most adults in Mongolia, was something she perceived as stressful.

'No,' she replied with a smile on her face. 'Actually, we find it enjoyable … I think Mongolians have historically got used to it.'

Oyunaa proceeded to explain why managing different tasks at the same time is something that she perceived that people enjoy:

> Rebecca, think of a single Mongolian herding family living in the middle of nowhere. Each family member has their own tasks that they are in charge of. These are all very different jobs. The wife may cook, clean, take care of children, collect dung and herd small animals and milk them. For one single person there are so many tasks to tend to.[3] And while people are used to being in charge of many different tasks, they are also used to the idea that these change seasonally. People are constantly planning at least one season ahead. For example, when at the summer pasture we have to think, if the summer goes well, then this will be the case, but if the summer does not go so well, then we need to make these changes to our plans.

Planning one step ahead, while accommodating uncertainty and change, is, according to Oyunaa, a feature of the way nomadic herding households manage their seasonal tasks. They are constantly in a process of approximating a model, or a predicted cycle, while adapting to that cycle as the seasons unfold.

Although this comparison sounded logical, I was somewhat surprised by Oyunaa's analogy. The 'vagaries of neoliberal capitalism' and nomadic herding practices are, in many ways, not at all similar. The focus on adapting to change, however, brought to mind the now widespread development term 'resilience', and what Evans and Reid (2014) have called the inherent 'bounce-back-ability' needed when the state has withdrawn its services. The term 'resilience' was first used to talk about the ability of an ecosystem to respond to a shock or disturbance by resisting damage and recovering quickly, something probably familiar among pastoral nomads, and began to gain popularity in international development after the 2008 food, fuel and financial crises left people searching for new approaches to tackling poverty.

The comparison also sounded familiar in another sense. One civil society leader, for example, explained in detail to me the likeness between surviving economic precariousness and nomadic herding:

> [One] of the core skills that any nomadic herder must possess is the ability to adjust quickly to the given environment. Since their entire life depends on the health of their livestock, herders must possess the ability to adjust quickly to Mongolia's sudden shifts in temperature, conditions of the pastureland, and vastly different environment/topography.

He reflected further,

> I think there are both great benefits and detrimental aspects associated with the ability to assimilate into any context, the biggest downside in my opinion being that Mongolians are quick to adjust to living in a bad environment – such as Ulaanbaatar, where corruption is rampant, air pollution is alarming and congestion is almost unbearable – and become content with their current situation rather than trying to change their surroundings and environment for the better.

It seemed that people from many different walks of life were comparing the skills and practices of nomadic herding to the way people in Mongolia were adapting to economic uncertainty. They used this analogy as *a form of self-description*. It allowed them to reflect on their current activities while also coming to terms with the disappointment of previous predictions having failed to materialise.

In many ways this analogy presents a parody of what nomadic life is like; I have to admit that I did not hear my friends in the countryside using this comparison (see Chapters 4 and 5). The reference by many in the city to 'adaptive nomadism' as a way of weathering change does, however, play into certain widespread nationalist overtones about what makes Mongolians distinct, strong and able to counter any storm. Many consider themselves to have an innate, or essential, characteristic of being able to withstand harsh environmental and economic climates (see the example from Ganbaatar in the Introduction, pp. 8–9).

Through these examples we can see that what we might assume from the outside to be incredibly stressful, precarious and uncertain ways of living are not always thought of in these terms. Attending to the idea that adaptation is valued as a national trait does not, of course, validate the deep structural inequality that exists in Mongolia across many different strata of society. However, by focusing on adaptability as a positive trait, many Mongolians seem to be illuminating how people can *reflect on and valorise their ability to adapt and survive*, making a life for themselves and their families within this environment. Oyunaa and Tüvshin's recovery, albeit gradual, from the collapse of the party business is to be celebrated. They never wanted to dwell for too long on a negative outcome. Their recovery provides an allegorical lesson – almost in the form of a classical epic – of how to adjust and find one's feet again in a place that one must come to understand anew.

Adaptation and resilience

Oyunaa's party business highlights a situation where one assumes the future is something clear and defined. A singular entity. Something that one can strive towards. This view is a linear and progressive idea of how people orient themselves towards the future. The failure of certain dreams to materialise along this defined path is attributed to the gap that exists between the 'dream' and the 'present condition' that makes it impossible for that dream to be realised. This failure is attributed by Oyunaa and others to the brute transplantation of models from elsewhere that don't fit the conditions in which they find themselves.

In contrast, futures perceived within the framework of 'nomadic adaptation' *emerge* as people revise previous visions of the future according to new ones. Here the future is constantly shifting and changing as the present *unfurls*. It becomes clearer the closer we get to it and, even then, multiple futures are often held in view at the same time as people hedge their bets on different outcomes. This is similar to what Pedersen has described as a 'multi-temporal attitude', where, '[r]ather than demonstrating a lack of interest in the future, living for the moment involves an exalted awareness of the virtual potentials in the present – the tiny but innumerable cracks through which the promise of another world shines' (Pedersen 2012, 10). It is important to point out that these cracks may be viewed simultaneously, and at other times they may also flicker in and out of view, some cancelling out others. This oscillation of different futures mirrors the oscillation in juggling various economic activities which permeates so many people's lives. In attending to these two temporalities we may say that there are

> those who imagine the future as a road ahead of them, stretching into the distance, and those for whom the future already hides in their surroundings, jumping out to everyone's surprise, where you never know what is going to appear or who is going to walk through the door next. (Strathern 2015, 124)

In 2016 the government was preoccupied with impending elections and how it would repay its massive public debts: it was looking squarely at the future as a road ahead. This led many to feel that the state was neglecting the economic and political concerns of its populace, the future hiding in the midst of the here and now. Being subject to such neglect, and often without legal protection and support when things went wrong, people were forced to adapt to and work around the hurdles in their paths.

In spite of this, many did not feel that the need to juggle several different things at once had simply been *imposed on them by the state*. It was obvious that many ordinary people had a sense of opportunity. Juggling several different business ventures and projects allowed a hedging of bets and provided a kind of insurance against failure (see Chuluunbat and Empson 2018).

Recall that Oyunaa was very keen to refute the idea that her existence should be seen as stressful. We are invited thereby to attend to the kinds of lives that are being forged in this context. A focus on the 'suffering of subjects', to use Robbins's term (2013), united through a 'shared sense of catastrophe', often obscures *the ways* in which people imagine and act

in the world to *open up new possibilities*. It often ignores the attempts people do make, on a daily basis, to *prefigure new futures* and move within
the political and economic environments they find themselves in. In this
sense Oyunaa's concept of 'adaptive nomadism' is very different from the
idea of resilience outlined by Evans and Reid (2014). It is not necessarily
about insecurity and vulnerability, but also about opportunity, chance
and luck and the ability to *spread one's assets across a range of different
activities* while hedging one's bets on multiple outcomes – or futures – at
the same time.

The economy of favours and the hedging of bets

Despite widespread political and economic uncertainty, people seemed
to voice recurring hope about the present. They continued to act as if
'tomorrow will be a better day by stubbornly making new debts and
entering into new trading ventures' (Pedersen 2012, 2) with seemingly
irrational optimism. One reason for this may be that, although many of
the different businesses that people are balancing may not bring financial
rewards, such activities do allow them to gain in *other ways*. Instead of
seeing this 'constant search for luck and its failure to materialise' as a feature of the predatory power of capitalism, we can discern a different kind
of explanation, one that the people themselves may offer.

In short, to class these activities as failures – and relegating their
outcomes to the vagaries of predatory capitalism – is probably to miss
an ethnographic insight into what exactly these activities do generate in
terms of the economy and the people involved. Humphrey (2012) has
focused on the term 'economy of favours', prominent in sociological
writings that discuss cronyism, social capital and corruption (Ledeneva
2006). What exactly the personal connections in this economy consist
of, she argues, is never really studied. 'Favours', she argues – using the
term to refer to a range of different phenomena – are not just indicative of
economic shortages or practical problems, such as disorder in legal and
political situations. Economies of favour are, in fact, often *outside the economic logic* of profit-driven exchange and persist beyond times of scarcity
and disorder (Henig and Makovicky 2017).

As highlighted by Zelizer (2010) and others, sentiments of various
kinds are attached to transactions and activities. To understand exactly
what sentiments these are, we need to focus on the structures that channel and control economic flows. Doing this, Humphrey argues, 'enables
us to conceptualise actions that have economic effect without themselves

having to be seen in terms of exchange' (Humphrey 2012, 26). Granting informal credit, barter, gift-giving and hospitality can all be viewed as structures that channel economic flows in Mongolia, because they are often ways to embed oneself in networks (Humphrey and Sneath 1999). In many of these activities people may not actually aspire to economic transactions *void of social relations*. They may instead be 'used to, prefer and value highly acting in this way' (Humphrey 2012, 24), where social relations are as much a part of the exchange as money and objects. In this context one might note that the reason for granting a favour is not simply for the immediate return it may bring. Rather, and here I follow Humphrey (2012), it allows the giver to maintain a moral supremacy, leaving the actor a creditor, should the occasion ever arise, but with no direct obligation to return the favour. Here we can see how favours are not transactional in an economic sense, but are based on the ad hoc activities of everyday life.[4]

Value placed on social relations maintained through the economy of favours points to a particular kind of shared morality. This, Humphrey argues, is an aesthetic of action that *endows actors with social standing and a sense of self-worth* (i.e. they are incalculable). These kinds of social interactions are what David Sneath (2006) has termed 'enactments', a major feature of which is their ability to *materialise social relations in particular ways*. An example from Mongolia might be the great attention given to the setting up of shareholders in a business. Attention to the distribution of shares among a group of people (like a kind of collective ownership) seems, in many instances, to override attention as to whether the activity will actually reap profitable rewards. The pervasive idea of collective entitlement to a shared portion (or shareholdership) in Mongolia is exemplified in business, the distribution of national profit, and usufructuary land ownership, whereby people *hold relations, networks and alliances in place* through such exchanges. Local understandings about the efficacy of such activities, therefore, disrupt normative views of economic models with other visions of what counts as a positive or successful outcome.

In this context people constantly implicate themselves in different chains of exchange for different kinds of goods and services. What they may be doing in juggling these different transactions, then, may not just be about profit – although that is, of course, a major drive. They are also expanding their sphere of contacts, *diversifying* their *social* as well as *material assets*. This is similar to what Pedersen has referred to as the 'work of hope' in the creation of social trust, 'necessary for the reproduction of socio-economic networks in Mongolia' (Pedersen 2012, 12).

It is essential to maintain such networks, not least because they allow one to believe that one may, one day, benefit from them. The failure of some of these activities to work out in the way they have been imagined, not least in their economic outcomes, does not seem to dissuade people from trying again, reconfiguring their goals so that the 'afterlife of hope' (to use Miyazaki's 2006 term) *is transfigured into something else*. This making of 'worlds within worlds' is perhaps similar to what Zigon (2014) has described in his work on communities in Vancouver as *'worlds of becoming'*. That is, the exchange of services or favours within existing networks provides entry points into a whole range of other things. The temporary – or maybe suspended – nature of these 'worlds' or entry points, he says, *is something that is inbuilt in them*. Grounded in openness, they always become *otherwise*.

One might think of loan and barter arrangements based on different chains of indebtedness in Mongolia in exactly this way – that is, as worlds not closed unto themselves or directed towards a fixed and known future but opening up possible *entry points to other things*. For many, engaging in these activities generates effects beyond the immediate world they inhabit.[5] Whereas there is an apathy towards the performative rhetoric of the state inviting people to spend and to establish businesses, people have instead turned inwards to prefigure their own futures through these kinds of multiple transactions within various networks. Here political life is visible not through forms of state power but through forms of exchange and the enacting of favours, maintaining chains of indebtedness and repayment, any one of which may open up a path towards something different. In many ways Oyunaa and Tüvshin's party business failed to recognise this important point. It was built out of their savings and didn't rely on others.

To focus on these kinds of practices as *opening up connections* rather than holding people in endless chains of debt is also to suspend moral judgement about what is good or considered a successful outcome (see Robbins 2013). By attending to the way that chances people take in their daily lives have positive outcomes we challenge our own versions of the real and give the aspirational and idealising aspects of the lives of others a place in our accounts, allowing us to hear how people on the margins of the state imagine better ways to live (see Robbins 2013, 459).

Past futures and their presences

I have focused on the way in which people create different futures for themselves through an economy of favours. One reason Oyunaa defends her positive attitude towards what may, at first, appear to be an uncertain existence can be encapsulated in the Mongolian saying 'if your attitude is good, then so too is your fate' (*sanaa zöv bol zayaa zöv*). From this perspective, life is always determined by a range of different factors that lie outside your control, but it is also what you make it. The idea that one needs to act as if one lives in the society one desires in order to bring that world into being resonates with the idea of prefigurative politics and the practice of prefiguring one's future as if it already exists (Graeber 2014). As mentioned in the Introduction, prefigurative speech acts are extremely prevalent in Mongolia, where the way one articulates the future in language is held to have an effect on the 'real' world outside linguistic utterance.

The irony of this kind of prefigurative language, as Graeber has astutely highlighted, is that there is always a gap between the future imagined and the future that is experienced. In this slippage a retroactive logic tends to erase past visions so that the present seems like the only logical outcome. A similar kind of perspective is prevalent where people see the present economic downturn as something they have to *work within* in order to forge their own future. Graeber refers to this inevitable future as the 'paradox of performativity', where one may hope for one kind of future outcome but something else happens, and in the time it takes for this outcome to happen it ceases to matter anymore. This slippage between a future imagined and the future realised calls to mind Nielsen's captivating phrase 'collapsed futures'. Whereas for Graeber the paradox is that no one remembers past futures, for Nielsen 'collapsed futures' refers to the way in which past futures 'manifest themselves as figurations of something that can never be but that, nevertheless, seem to structure the temporal orientation of the present as a retrograde and mobile moment of origin' (Nielsen 2014, 217).

For people like Oyunaa and Tüvshin, past futures have mostly been erased in favour of new ones, even if these, like the concept of nomadic adaptability, reach back further in time to a past that jumps, or maybe leaps from a distant time, into the present.[6] What vision or value is retained from the past and what is new and transplanted are difficult to disentangle in current articulations, which are themselves born from the ability to step outside one's current life and reflect on it through such analogies. We have seen how people juggle different futures through various economic endeavours. Rather than see these as somehow outside, or counter to, mainstream economic practices (based on the accumulation of profit), I suggest they are shaping the current form of the economy in Mongolia. By following the way that Oyunaa and her husband managed to make a life for themselves after their business collapsed and were able to find a more 'sustainable way of life', as Oyunaa put it, I suggest that we may also find ways to let people's own efforts and practices inform anthropological understanding of these worlds.

Reflection

In examining how people live through the failure of economic predictions on a national scale, I have focused on two areas of concern. Firstly, I have looked at the way in which some dreams are often quite divorced from the context in which they can be realised, be this wider economic policies based on models developed elsewhere or individual business ventures transplanted from other places. This divorce is highlighted in the concept of the gap, which exists between people's visions of the future and the reality that would enable those visions to materialise. Focusing on the idea of the gap has allowed me to explore the paradox of performativity and the way in which people erase past futures once they have failed to materialise. In exploring this paradox, we see that running a large party business in Mongolia was a reality that, for many reasons, could not be sustained. A mismatch existed between the vision and the reality, between the figure or exemplar imagined and the ground on which it could flourish.

I hope that it has become apparent that my ethnographic focus alludes to a similar mismatch that exists for Mongolia as a country, with the mining boom and its subsequent collapse. When GDP was soaring, the government took out huge loans, banking on their ability to repay them within a few years. Dreams were speculated and risks were taken, driven by advice based on models from elsewhere. Nowadays inactivity has taken hold as commodity prices have dropped and foreign investors have left. Just as the apartment was left full of party supplies, so does Mongolia's territory contain untapped resources that are slowly being syphoned off at cut-price rates to China, to repay looming debts. Each description could be read as an analogy for the other, even if it remains to be seen how Mongolia as a nation will adapt to this gap.

Secondly, I have focused on the way in which the gap allows people to reflect on their ability to juggle different futures, revising and changing them according to the way things turn out, all the while coping with the multiple chains of indebtedness that allow these suspended futures to exist. Their ability to do this, some argue, is down to an ability to adapt to situations as they emerge. Although some may argue that this is no more than a nationalist-essentialist caricature that romanticises nomadic herding, one gets the sense that in such self-reflection – however essentialist it may be – Mongolians are at once *celebrating their resourcefulness as well as explaining to themselves how they have come to internalise a future that did not approximate what was predicted.*

These two areas of focus have illuminated two distinct temporalities: one, goal-oriented and singular, but never occurring in the way it is imagined (the party business based on formal loans); the other, fluid and changing, and often used as a way to critique the first. Here innovation emerges from working within existing structural logics, based on personal loans and counter-loans through individuals held in a network, and sharing portions out among a group of people who hold each other in place through facilitating each other's projects (see Chuluunbat and Empson 2018). Although defenders (of performativity) might say that these visions do structure action, recent critiques of performative economics have shown that these are never seamless processes; there is always a slippage, or gap, between the future imagined and the experience of that future. Not only is there often a slippage or gap, but people may hold multiple visions of the future in mind simultaneously. As Nielsen notes for Mozambique, 'the financial "success story" covers only a few sectors and benefits only a small elite minority while leaving behind the large and impoverished majority' (Nielsen 2014, 220).

Certainly, a renewed belief in the present helped Oyunaa and Tüvshin to reorient past dreams. In the way they did this we can see the 'lived futures that emerge in the "gap" in the temporal doxa' (Guyer 2007, 411) between past and future. These 'lived futures' are not 'outside' the dominant economy. Rather, people are continually oscillating in and out of different kinds of economic activities and in doing so they productively engage with and perform the different futures they seek. In this dialectic, between visions of the future that determine activities and the activities themselves determining people's futures, we can begin to see the complex ways in which future dreams are always *folded into* present activities as one vision replaces another, never completely materialising before another begins to takes shape.

The argument that economic and political temporal imaginaries are often framed in terms of unilinear progression is always an imposition: a model or vision that papers over a multitude with a notion of singularity; a straw man that anthropologists have long sought to expose and could be argued to be the basis of substantivist critique. However, renewed hope in progress is often what drives political and economic reform, even if we know that futures are multiple and embedded in dense temporalities.

This return to singularity undoubtedly creates an underlying element of doubt in people's lives, leading to a hedging of bets, whereby different possible future outcomes are kept alive as possibilities, just in case one or other drops by the wayside. In a sense, maintaining this element of doubt is a form of political critique. It allows people to suspend their judgement about the way things will turn out and spread their losses over a range of different projects and ideas as they adapt to events in the unfurling of time. Holding different horizons in place so that a singular, idealised vision of the future is deferred, allowing multiple possible outcomes in its place, is both a form of resistance and a way to bring things into being.

Notes

1. This was one of the only people I met in person who had defaulted on a loan and actually had collateral seized, rather than have the repayment schedule extended, although people did frequently recount that this had happened to others (see Chapter 5).
2. It is common for many people in their forties and fifties to have worked for some time as a husband-and-wife team.
3. Oyunaa elaborated that 'Mongolian children take care of toddlers, collect water, firewood, and keep their eyes on small animals. You know, for a Mongolian woman going to the outhouse involves checking everything on her way there and back – is the family secure? is everything the way it should be? – all the while tidying up, cleaning, collecting animal dung, looking after animals and things. Mongolians are used to managing multiple tasks at the same time.'
4. Humphrey notes, 'At some moments favors initiate and open out new ties, while at others, particularly when these favors are illegal or seen formally as somehow corrupt, they tend to restrict networks and turn them into closed circles' (Humphrey 2012, 25).
5. For example, when a man pawns his car to take out a loan so that his brother may invest in a new business, this money may, in fact, be used for a range of other things, like paying off previous debts or lending to those who have previously been a source of cash. All the while repayments are required on the loan in order to pay back your brother so that he may have his car back. Here social relations are being maintained so that access to future wealth may be kept open as a possibility, even if that possibility may never be realised.
6. They are in a sense 'pre-existing' what has not yet happened (and will probably never happen) and cannot form a clear image or map of the future (see Pedersen 2012, 9).

Interlude I

Ulaanbaatar is dusty, bleak and windy. Waiting for the bus, I am forced to seek momentary refuge in a KFC doorway, when, out of nowhere, the sky turns an ominous brownish yellow. High-speed wind torpedoes through the city and lashes my body, filling my nose and mouth with dust. I haven't yet learnt the art of always wearing a scarf around my neck to protect against such moments. The climate is unpredictable and so is the political atmosphere. Like political life itself, the storm appears to come out of nowhere.

It is early May 2016 and there is still some ice on the main river that runs through the city (the Tuul). Snow can be seen on the mountains to the south. Workmen are starting to put down new pavements and are planting trees along the roadsides. The news reports that the police are undergoing crash courses in English. Everything must be in place for ASEM (the eleventh Asia–Europe Meeting). In contrast, deserted construction projects lie in wait for new investment and small shops are getting rid of stock before they close down, with sales offering 30–40 per cent discounts. Rumours spread that a measles epidemic has erupted and infant mortality is spiralling out of control across the city. No doubt the government will hide all of this from its foreign visitors when they arrive later in the summer.

With the so-called 'economic crisis' two things have become apparent: while the rich are stuck with unfinished property and dormant mining licences they cannot act on, the poor have lots of cheap goods – now mostly broken and used for something else – that they bought on credit and still have to pay for. Everyone talks about debt and its vast accumulation. It is certain that the Democratic Party will not be re-elected, but who will take their place? Will it be a coalition? Will any of the independent candidates be elected? What of the new and emerging parties? Why do they seem to implode through internal factions?

In the afternoon of 4 May I receive an SMS message from a friend that a Mercedes-Benz has just driven past a bus stop in the centre of town and thrown hundreds of thousands of tögrög *out of the window at people wait-ing for the bus. Could this be a political move related to the elections? Is it just the tip of the iceberg of many more such events? If so, who is the man in the car? Through what connections has he got hold of such large amounts of cash? By the end of the day, and on (apparent) police investigation, it is con-firmed that this was simply the action of a man who had been arguing with his wife. The speculations die out and the event is soon forgotten.*

On 11 April a prominent politician and businessman's offices are raided, an event presumed to have to do with the ongoing 'railway scandal', in which miles and miles of purchased tracks have been left to rust on the steppe. A large group of people, including the national judo team and var-ious politicians, come out to support him. Special forces police officers can be seen live on TV, seizing boxes and taking them away, but the man is never arrested himself. 'We're just really living in a society where the law is no longer the law,' his daughter laments. Speculation about internal factions aside, in this gesture we are reminded that the state holds ultimate power.

After the event, rumours circulate about future arrests and a list that has been drawn up with the names of those who might be targeted next. At night, people have been seen trying to sell their Tavan Tolgoi (the world's third-biggest coking coal deposit) government-allocated shares to eager Chinese buyers (shares the government later agreed to buy back). During the day the flow of life is intermittently halted by the stopping of traffic to allow blacked-out cars with sirens to dart past carrying ASEM-related visitors at speed through the city.[1] The façades of buildings along the main roads are being painted and motorway shoulders are being raised to hide unsightly slums. The political atmosphere is characterised by a sense of fits and starts: things suddenly emerge as if from nowhere and are followed by a period of intense speculation and a search for connections and comprehension. Then, just as quickly, they dissipate into the background again and things return to some sense of normalcy.

As the weather warms, the Tuul begins to thaw. In the mornings men and women, sometimes with children in tow, come to gather plastic bottles along its banks, carrying them home in woven plastic bags on their backs. Sometimes these people travel by bus, sitting awkwardly with their enormous luggage slipping across the floor into the elites who use the route to travel from their exclusive villas into the city centre. As it gets warmer I walk across the river and up into the mountains beyond. A small trickle of water appears but, instead of this leading to a large torrent, a few days later the water disappears completely. People speculate that the government has syphoned off part of the river to provide water for the new ASEM buildings being built for the foreign visitors. Two days later, however, the river begins to flow as the ice thaws fur-ther up in the mountains, and just as suddenly the speculation disappears.

*These events hint at the way in which politics is discussed in Mongolia –
as rumours about the motives of politicians and businessmen, rather than
discussion about policy. The drying up of the Tuul and the rumours that
surrounded it, as well as the lack of interest when the actual reason was
revealed, is just one example. In the lead-up to the parliamentary elections
of 2016, people were constantly searching for meaning – connections and
explanations – in actions they found difficult to read and understand. In
fact, this searching for meaning and speculation is* what politics is. *It is the
speculation about connections and motivations beyond the visible and tan-
gible. To understand politics – or to* think politics *– is to understand the
underside of things, beyond the way things appear to the ordinary eye, to
uncover the workings of a kind of magic or religion.*

*'Nothing can be understood', one friend recounted, 'if the networks
underneath are not known and understood.' He elaborated further, 'If you
don't understand the motivations of individuals then politics in Mongolia is
impossible to understand.'*

*Searching for the motivation behind actions that seem strange is some-
times the only way people are able to process the wayward atmosphere that
seems to characterise so much of political life here. And though the new,
younger politicians are seen as potentially hopeful (they don't have, as yet,
such a trail of speculated exchange of favours attached to them), they are all
locked within the dominant parties and have little room to make a mark.
It is as if, with the politicians tightly held within alliances of debt and obligation, there is no room for new political visions to emerge. Everything is
understood as driven by personal gains that bind people to each other, con-
straining as well as determining actions.*

*In this atmosphere, politics appears a kind of empty shell. People feel
they are living in an economic system (capitalism) rather than a political
one (democracy now appears jaded and opaque). Because the economic
system persists regardless of who is in charge, politics as an intervention
appears defunct, a point that makes attaching the term 'crisis' to the word
'economic' a kind of political parody (see Roitman 2014). In this light, we
might ask what work the term 'crisis' does in narratives about the economy in
Mongolia. From one perspective it appears to be a political move to try to contain the moment in a specific temporal framework; the idea that crisis is an
event is of course exposed as a fallacy when it is realised to be the norm. Here
the norm, the ordinary, is the speculation and incoherence of political life.
The economic crisis is not an exception. There is, in many ways, a sense of a
'crisis ordinary', of 'a process embedded in the ordinary that unfolds in stories
about navigating what is overwhelming' (Berlant 2011, 10). Perhaps politics
is not such an empty shell after all. In these ways of navigating sometimes*

overwhelming relations of debt, both monetary and social, and the complex entangled relations of obligation and favour that flow in their wake, life is always intensely political. It is just being played out in a different sphere from that which any election promises would have us believe it is.

Note

1. In what some might say was an aggressive electioneering policy, or a way to placate increasing unrest and critique, handouts of 20 per cent of shares in Tavan Tolgoi – the world's third-biggest coking coal deposit – were distributed among citizens. In May 2012, ahead of parliamentary elections, people were able to sell their stake back to the state for MNT1 million or keep the shares (Hook 2012). In 2016, when the economy was in crisis, they again tried to sell them (see Yeung and Howes [2015, 13–15] for more details).

Figure 2 'Air' *Agaar*, by Nomin Bold, 2019. Acrylic, canvas 245 × 145 cm.

2
Democracy and its discontent

In the autumn of 2015 I find myself at a hotel in Ulaanbaatar, at an exclusive birthday party for a friend. She has hired two rooms on the ground floor. The first has a long table, at which we gather – couples and friends who have known each other for a lifetime – to be served a lavish three-course meal. In the second, a live band set up and begin to play. As the evening progresses, the lights are dimmed and the wine from the meal continues as we move next door. We sit, as has become familiar at such events, on chairs along the walls and wait to dance in pairs. Only, by now we are all women and we dance with each other, in different styles to different kinds of music, and then there is a competition as to which pair dances best to which style of music. I am in a cashmere dress I bought from a factory outlet store, with woollen tights and long boots. Inappropriately warm attire for dancing with Sara, an old friend of the woman whose birthday we are celebrating.

As the evening turns into early morning, I catch a lift in a blacked-out four-by-four with one of the women whose private driver has been waiting outside. She's in her early fifties, works at a bank, is immaculately dressed and clutches a Chanel handbag. I get out at my building, where my son is asleep inside. I feel fortunate to have been included in this celebration as part of the inner circle of an old friend whom I have known for years and whose birthday has happened to coincide with my visit.

This chapter explores the way in which people in Mongolia articulate their discontent with the current political and economic climate. In particular, they are looking for alternatives to the system of politics that was adopted in the democratic revolution of the early 1990s. Through the example of one woman we see how the rapid economic changes of the past few years have opened up a space for her and her friends to reflect on the current state of politics. They look inwards and to the past for exemplary models of subjectivity. Whereas Mongolia as a nation often looks to the thirteenth century, to the period of Chinggis Khaan and the empire, for examples of successful ways of organising political life (see Dulam 2020; Kaplonski 2004), the ethnography explored here illuminates how people may do so on an individual basis, cultivating their thirteenth-century souls as exemplars for who they may become. This is a way of prefiguring oneself as a citizen for the nation.

Through this ethnography I argue that what may be dismissed as 'populist rhetoric' should actually be attended to and explored as a nuanced critique of the way neoliberal policies have been adopted in Mongolia and encouraged by foreign donors and investors. I draw on a range of works that, following Laclau (2005), show how populist critique can revitalise democratic processes, 'recalibrating' them to the needs of 'the people' they serve rather than simply challenge them. I suggest that we need to reflect more critically on the ideological baggage of the term 'populist' and its relationship with conflicting understandings of democracy.

*

My dance partner that evening was Sara, a tall, striking 50-year-old woman whom I have known for almost two decades. She is married to Ochir and together they have two daughters. Currently Sara runs a real estate company that has, since the late 2000s, benefited from the many foreign investors who came to the country needing apartments in the city. Since 2013, however, sales have been slow, if not non-existent. Whereas she used to employ six people, she now has only one part-time employee. In fact, as I came to realise over the course of 2014–16, their office is mostly a front for holding meetings with a group of people and their spiritual leader, and their reading and discussion groups.

Graduating from university in Novosibirsk in 1991 with a degree in geology and engineering, Sara went straight into a job at the Ministry of Geology. But life was tough, and in the early 1990s she began to run a small grocery shop on the side, importing non-perishable food items wholesale from Russia and making a small profit from their resale. Not wanting to spend her life as a trader, she did a master's in public administration at the Management Institute in Ulaanbaatar. One of her teachers there offered her work as an assistant to a member of the Social Democratic Party, and from 1996 she worked in parliament, as an assistant to an MP and then as secretary of the Standing Committee. 'At that time politicians were normal people, not like the monsters they are now,' she comments.

Imagining a future life in politics, in 1999 she studied for two years for a master's in diplomacy at Westminster University, London, while her daughter went to school and her husband worked in various restaurants and as a cleaner. On her return to Mongolia, in 2002, she worked for the United Nations Development Programme (UNDP) and the Ministry of Foreign Affairs, overseeing the organisation of a large conference with more than 600 foreign participants. In the autumn of 2003 she started work at the Ministry of Roads, Transport and Tourism, where she stayed until 2008.

Given her background – her experience in government and her exposure to other countries – in 2008 Sara took a chance and decided to run as an MP in the parliamentary elections. Like many MPs, she ran her real estate business in the evenings and worked at the Ministry during the day (at the time, she comments, all politicians had two or three businesses alongside their civil jobs). In the end she wasn't elected, but it was during this period in her life that she began to question what politics was:

> [I] saw increasingly that unqualified people were working in the Ministry and [I] began to think about what [I] could do for Mongolia. The reason I ran for politics is that I wanted to contribute to my country, but I now realise that no one can make a change; it is the system which is wrong.

From 2008 to 2013, as the economy heated up, it was perhaps a blessing that, instead of a life in parliament, she was able to focus on considerably expanding her real estate business. She comments that during this time investors in the property market were mostly politicians, who had the advantage of being able to claim land to build on illegally. But when we talked in April 2016 she had only made one sale since December 2015.

> All the construction companies are now heavily in debt and need to pay back their bank loans. People are forced to buy unfinished buildings and they don't exchange sales with money. Instead they barter one kind of building for another.

Between 2010 and 2012 business was different, she explains. They were selling two properties a month and renting to foreign mining companies. By mid-2013 things had slowed down and sales were mostly between Mongolians. Sara's experience of working in politics and her real estate business has allowed her a unique insight into economic and political life.

A few months after the birthday party described at the start of this chapter, I met Sara in a bar in the centre of town. It was 2016 and I noticed she had become increasingly political, some might even say nationalistic. While we sat together at a table, her friend handed me her mobile phone to type something into the search engine. Having recently taken a long-haul flight from Moscow, on which such phones were banned, I looked at it and asked, 'Wow, is this the kind of Samsung that blows up?'[1] Sara smiled and immediately replied, 'No, it's only in America that it does that.' Her response put her political allegiance squarely in Asia, where the US and its idea of democracy were considered to be consolidating against Asians. Belonging to a generation of people in Mongolia who are tired of the promises and language of democracy, Sara commented flatly (while her friend grinned nervously), 'Perhaps now that Trump has been elected America will begin to manage its own business, rather than bomb the hell out of other places and colonise others with its neoliberal ideology.'

Somewhat shocked, I also felt excited by her frankness and her lack of formal etiquette that characterises so much of Mongolian social life. These women are educated, smart and proud to be Mongolian. They had travelled widely and had seen different places. But their politics had changed rapidly. Only a few years before they had boasted about making a shopping trip to Italy. Their current political outlook sat oddly with this consumerist past. Something had changed, or an aspect of them previously suppressed had now come to the fore.

Instead of to Italy, when I met her in 2016 Sara had just been on a research trip to the easternmost provinces of Mongolia. She showed me a video she had taken of huge hay fields covered in black bags of hay, gathered and sold to Chinese traders. She was furious. 'How are they allowed to come and buy our hay?' she stormed. When the state does not seem able to stop the actions of neighbouring nations to access local resources, this lack of ability to act leads to deep-felt frustrations (see Waters 2019).

Sara's previous work had allowed her insight into the way politics had come to be dominated by male business groups and patronage factions. The pervasiveness of such political groups leads Radchenko and Jargalsaikhan (2017) to ask why democracy persists in Mongolia, against the odds. They argue that although a strong parliament constrains the power of the presidency, this is not the only thing that upholds the democratic process. Instead 'the key feature that helps explain the Mongolian "aberration" is the existence of multiple interlinked patronage networks and rife factionalism, which causes dispersal of political power' (Radchenko and Jargalsaikhan 2017, 1035). These, they argue, serve as a constraint upon claims to power from an individual leader, so that factionalism prevents the build-up of power by one political party, thereby inadvertently helping to uphold democracy. Such factions also channel resources and business opportunities: 'Political parties are seen as a gateway for entrepreneurs to tap the state resources through tenders and loans' (Radchenko and Jargalsaikhan 2017, 1040). Business groups cut across party alliances so that '[r]ight, left, center – all of that hardly matters. The one thing that does matter is one's patronage network' (Radchenko and Jargalsaikhan 2017, 1053). Sara's insight into these networks and factions led her to comment angrily,

> Democracy is nothing; it is just bullshit. It is [a] new word that is completely empty. We chose it in the 1990s without knowing what it was, and as a consequence we've lost our land, our environment and our economic independence.

She went on to reflect on the deeply ingrained corruption prevalent among the political elite as a kind of 'black hole' (*har nüh*):

> Rebecca, you should see that it is only the banking system that is getting rich now, and behind the banks that are pocketing all our money are foreign investors. This is our 'black hole'. Mongolians are fighting away with each other while foreigners eat all our money.

This sense of Mongolia losing its resources to outsiders frequently triggers nationalist retort, defending innocent Mongolians from foreigners who want to pillage the country's resources.

Importantly, however, this critique was not just marshalled in 'us/them' terms, but also led to internal critique, of elite Mongolian politicians who were perceived to be self-serving rather than looking after the nation (see Introduction). Sara may possibly have been privy to some of these deals, since her work in the real estate market would have put her in contact with people who had purchased land for development in and around the restricted Bogd Haan National Park area, a practice that was critiqued later as serving only the wealthiest elites. In this light, Sara went on, there is the need for a new kind of political leader: 'While every Mongolian person wants to rise up and improve their lives, we also want a change. We don't want a dictator we have to follow and admire, but we do want a strong leader.'

The search for a new kind of political leader was partially answered in the 2017 presidential election. Battulga was elected as Mongolia's fifth president and is seen by many as a populist choice: he is extremely wealthy and a judo champion, with little experience in politics. He is outwardly critical of Mongolia's resources being controlled by a few politically con- nected businessmen and of the increasing income gap between the rich and the poor. This critique resonates with people, and his appointment was received by many as a breath of fresh air.

Although his 'public grievances against accumulation and dispos- session have been discounted as populist cries' (Myadar and Jackson 2018, 1) by some, particularly from the Democratic Party, labelling someone 'populist' often serves to silence critique and flattens the pos- sibility of examining its content. Indeed, Myadar and Jackson (2018) argue that Battulga's victory should be seen as an expression of a broader discontent driven by neoliberal reforms that began in Mongolia in the early 1990s with the feeling that outsiders were taking unfair advan- tage of Mongolia. This discontent, as we shall see, has a nationalist focus and is critical of the rapid economic change associated with the mining economy, democracy and the Democratic Party.

> Neoliberal policies have allowed the accumulation of wealth and power into the hands of a few – both domestic and foreign – whereas the majority have not benefited from Mongolia's mining riches but have had to bear more negative externalities. (Myadar and Jackson 2018, 1)

To counter these grievances, opponents, especially foreign investors, frame these critiques as 'resource nationalist' or 'populist' – both of which silence the range of objections to structural dispossession (Myadar and Jackson 2018).

Ancient wisdom and alternative exemplars

Later that month I met Sara again, but this time at her empty office, where our conversation took a somewhat different turn. Instead of criti- quing politicians for giving Mongolia's resources away to foreigners, she talked in more detail about the alternative exemplars she had begun to look towards for a better future for the country.

> To ease our lives, we have realised that we have to learn from Mongolian ancient wisdom to make our lives better. We have forgotten a lot of this knowledge because of socialism and Western influences.

We were cheap and short-sighted allowing them to dig here and destroy our ecosystem. Our individual human values have been lost during democracy, while our traditions were lost during socialism.

...

The parliament, the multi-party system, democracy is all rubbish. It disadvantages Mongolian people again and again. The politicians just care about themselves and are short-sighted, signing off the country to foreign mining companies. We have tried to live in the four-year cycle of parliamentary elections but the cycle is too short, and policy is hard to implement. Now people realise that democracy is a bad experiment and doesn't really exist perfectly anywhere. When I came back from the UK I realised democracy was just an experiment and its results were not good. At first people thought I was crazy, but now they have begun to see it for themselves. Everyone is just concerned with earning money. We have been forced under economic pressure to think solely about our bank loans and mortgages, leaving no space for any other thoughts.

I was struck by the way Sara articulated so succinctly current political discontent, not just here in Mongolia, but globally. Her theorising of politics and her search for an 'alternative route' highlighted that things needed to change, that late capitalism had come to an end: that we had reached a tipping point and new social forms were desired. 'During [the] socialist period we had over 800 industries here, now we have maybe five, the rest are in ruins,' she lamented.

At the moment we have lost several kinds of independence: economic independence, national independence, territorial independence, state independence, and independence of mind. ... This democratic system is wrong. It disadvantages Mongolian people and politicians and makes them believe that the only purpose in life is to get rich.

A few months later I met Sara at her house with her daughters. It is an intimate occasion. I know the evening will be a long one and will involve sharing about personal things while making food together. The day before, I attended her private reading group, where I met one of its members, a woman who works at the Asia Development Bank during the day and channels Attila the Hun at night, along with the nine white spirits and the four seasons (see Interlude 4). The group is composed of 15–20 people who are all followers of a woman called Gerel, who reveals your ancient 'soul' from the thirteenth century. She has 'woken the souls of 1181 people', or 'kings and queens', in order to 'awaken Mongolia' again and influence the whole world. 'Together, if we follow the path outlined by this woman', Sara almost whispers, 'things will change'.

The reading group was first formed in 2012 and may be viewed as a sub-group of this larger group of followers of Gerel. At the moment, they gather weekly to discuss a text produced by Gerel while in trance, which they refer to as the 'Secret History of the Mongols Before It Was Translated into Chinese'. The text is almost incomprehensible to readers of standard Mongolian and is understood to be in some ancient dialect of Mongolian that requires a lot of deciphering. Discussing and analysing the meaning of the text is performative. Doing so enacts a way of being – gathering, talking, evaluating, discussing – things the group members would like to dominate their lives outside this context. It is a kind of communal translation activity and an uncovering of knowledge for a new universe, a coming into being of prophecy and metaphysical speculation.[2] It is a means by which they question the existing order of things and try to bring into view a different kind of world.

They also use this text to discuss a broad range of issues: how to act morally, what allegorical lessons may be learnt from the stories, but also how things should be managed politically and collectively. The group members see themselves as part of a movement to 'awaken' people to the true way of being Mongolian subjects.

As the evening progresses, I learn that within this group Sara has been granted a high title. In the historical past, she was, according to their belief, a high-ranking queen in an area of western Mongolia. She explains that in the granting of such titles the members are being invited to *setgel sereh* – to 'raise their spirit/feeling/psychological outlook' in a world that seems broken and corrupt. She shows me the costume she wears during meetings, which includes elaborate hats. Through coming to learn about her past self, she explains, she is learning how to be an exemplary mother, wife, daughter-in-law and leader – skills that have been lost because of the corrupt morality of socialism and democracy.

Her work is very busy, since she has lots she needs to learn and study, both for herself and for others; she is trying to master the skill of reading people's souls. This is one of the reasons she needs 800 sheep ankle bones, of which I've contributed 20 as my visiting gift. Unsurprised at the convergence of her husband's interest in history with her own interest in politics, I leave her house that evening feeling like I've become privy to the early articulations of a new form of prefigurative politics and critique. Coming to know one's ancient soul person entails coming to know who one can be, while also being given a 'role', a 'costume' and a position among a wider group of people, literally allowing one to bring that person into being in the present.

Later that week I have the great fortune to meet Gerel at Sara's office. Before she arrives, there is a very excitable and slightly anxious atmosphere. I pop out to improve my outfit and to purchase a formal gift and a ceremonial silk scarf in which to give it. Sara's husband is pacing the room and there are a few other colleagues and relatives also eager to meet Gerel. Suddenly she arrives: a small, neatly dressed lady in a silk suit with her hair up, flanked by two bulky men talking on mobile phones. I greet her with respect and hand her a ceremonial silk scarf and chocolates. The others in the room refer to her as 'Honourable Enlightened Teacher' *Gegeenten Bagsh* or 'Brain with the Key to the Heavenly Mandate' (*Mönh tengeriin on's*).

We sit down at a large table, me and her on one side, the others opposite us. Three years ago, she explains, she was a kindergarten teacher in the countryside, but now her mission is to locate the souls of 1181 kings and queens of Mongolia in order to awaken Mongolia and influence the whole world. The decree granted to her will continue for nine years. So far she has worked for four years, the first three of which she was quiet.

But now, for over a year, she has been interacting with the public because 'it is the right time to do so'. She goes on to explain how she came to be able to read people's souls and explains her mission to build up a new state for Mongolia, 'closing the three doors to hell' with the 'help of 1181 people' whose 'souls have all been traced'. 'The three doors to hell (one in India, one in Egypt and one in Mongolia) need to be closed', to 'cleanse the universe', a task that can only be completed by her followers. Only when everyone comes together will Mongolia prosper and rise. Her job is to inform people of their past lives, to 'awaken people's belief in themselves and to give their lives purpose'.

The second part of our meeting begins, almost without my noticing, as she tunes in like a radio switching channels and talks about my past soul. She elaborates on this in great detail without stopping and provides countless bits of information that cause the people in the room to smile and nod at me with approval. I am drawn in by the complex details of the character she describes and begin to take notes. Just as suddenly as she began she stops, taking only a moment to adjust her hair clips slightly before commencing readings for two other people. Exchanging some formalities with Sara and her husband about events taking place in the coming days, she leaves, flanked by her bodyguards.

An excitable atmosphere fills the room in her absence. We remain in our places and recall the information she gave to each of us, reflecting on the overall cosmology she subscribes to. Sara and her husband go over the details with me before they discuss arrangements for a large meeting they are hosting in a stadium tomorrow, involving more than a thousand people. We are lucky to witness this organising, since it is all highly secret and Gerel will not answer any questions about the event and neither will any of the others. Sara completes her work organising the meeting and then dashes out to tend to some other tasks for tomorrow. There is no sense that they should be working on their real estate business. This is their real work and what seems to preoccupy them.

I have deliberately detailed the way in which my time with Sara moved from her talking about her outward politics to her inner ideas and work. This was not inevitable but emerged as an outcome of the time we spent together. To some, Sara and her group may seem to be New Age spiritualists, searching for meaning in a world that is moving too quickly and appears to reward unevenly. Such a turn to religion and spirituality in times of upheaval does not seem to be unique (see Comaroff and Comaroff 1999). Anthropologists have argued that shamanism in Mongolia grew in the post-socialist period in 'reaction to' or as a way to 'comprehend' post-socialist 'shock therapy' (Buyandelger 2013; Pedersen 2011). Personally, I would see this not as expressing a wider discontent with democracy, but rather as something born out of a wider rejection of the way things currently are. Furthermore, and this is important to highlight, for people like Sara and those in her group, the work they are doing should not necessarily be considered 'religious'. What we may think of as spiritual is in fact deeply political and a guide for how to act in the world today.

Given her general interest in politics, history and society, Sara has begun to appear to me more as a modern kind of nationalist intellectual. What may seem inward and parochial appears to her and her peers as expansive and worldly, recognising their place in a wider cosmos. With their organised research trips, their weekly reading groups and the group meetings to discuss and enact their place in a new kind of Mongolia, Sara and her friends see themselves as politically engaged and forward-thinking. Their shared cosmology is a vehicle by which they can interpret the world around them and prefigure the kind of future they want to live in.[3]

Conflicting political visions

Others, particularly those who oversaw many of the rapid reforms of the mining boom, might label Sara's outlook 'populist', a term that in Mongolia originated during the Soviet period and was used to dismiss those who voiced anti-party views. Today the term 'populism' (*populizm*) is often used divisively by the government to silence critique of policies that seem to only benefit the few. They would claim that Sara's critique propagates ideology that goes against international relations and ideas of 'development', arguing that populists appeal to the lowest possible denominator and are out of touch with the wider demands of global capitalism.

Pitting local needs and concerns against wider sacrifices makes such voices small and insignificant. In relation to this, Giménez Aliaga calls 'for a more thorough reflection on the ideological load of the term populism [and] its relationship with conflicting understandings of democracy' (Giménez Aliaga 2017, 1). Cast as the enemy of liberal democracy and freedom, 'populism' often conflates disparate political projects under one conceptual category. When used by the Mongolian state against those who critique it, for example, it fosters an image of 'the people' as ignorant and uneducated, framing voices of political discontent as opponents of progress. It also points to a technocratic idea of power in which only the experts can decide on things.

When a term is used to silence heterogeneous forms of critique it masks more than it reveals. Anthropologists would do well to attend to the content of this critique, to how it came about and to what alternative futures such voices call for. Frequently, in Mongolia, these critiques are the only voices against the extraction of Mongolia's environmental resources for the fuelling of Chinese production of the cheap goods that people so rely on in the West. They are the only voices that articulate discontent with what they feel is the unfurling of an economic system that they have not chosen to take part in but is being forced upon them and does not recognise their needs in the system of change. As mentioned earlier, the election of Battulga in 2017 can be seen as the start of some kind of institutional change. His appointment was swiftly followed by the arrest and imprisonment of the previous democratic leaders, Saikhanbileg and Bayartsogt. In December 2018 critique of the political faction that seemed to have benefited most from the resource boom was further evident in a large public protest that called for the resignation of the Speaker of Parliament, who was held to have sold government positions for profit and channelled wealth to members of their faction. Mobile felt tents were pitched on the State Square. Hunger protests began and continued into 2019. However, this period coincided with IMF restrictions on the economy and austerity policies that reduced the power of the nation state.

It is in this context that critique of democracy as a colonial import was often voiced by people like Sara. However, what was being critiqued and who this critique was aimed at was not always obvious. Although insecurity and rapid economic change often gave rise to critique of foreigners and the political elites who could be unresponsive to the concerns of other citizens, leading to people who voiced such kinds of concerns being deemed 'populist'.

Perceptions of widespread corruption among elites also plays into critique that is labelled populist in Northern and Southern Europe, as well as in North America. Katsambekis (2017) defines 'populism' as something composed of two particular elements. On the one hand, populism is a discursive construction and interpretation of who constitutes 'the people' as a collective subject of social change. 'The people' are called upon as the only ones who can legitimise democratic decision-making. On the other hand, he argues, populist ideas are characterised by sharp antagonistic worldviews, creating divisions between the people and the establishment, the underdog and the elite, or the marginalised many and the privileged few. Here populists are held to serve the people and reinforce popular sovereignty, accountability and participation.

Through focusing on someone like Sara we may begin to reflect more critically on the ideological baggage of the term 'populist' and its relationship with conflicting understandings of democracy. Giménez Aliaga (2017) describes how, after years of economic crisis, austerity policies, lack of jobs and corruption scandals in Spain, the anti-austerity party Podemos rallied political discontent in 2014, drawing a host of different interest groups into politics. This form of populism was unrelated to the racism, xenophobia, misogyny and nationalism often associated with populist movements elsewhere. Instead, Aliaga argues, it is the kind of populism that Laclau, the Argentinian political theorist who pioneered the Essex School of discourse analysis, refers to as 'an empty signifier', able to gather different ideas and causes into it.

In *On Populist Reason* (2005) Laclau considers the nature of populism in political discourse, the creation of a popular hegemonic bloc such as 'the people' and the importance of affect in politics. He argues that the basis of populism lies in the creation of empty signifiers: words and ideas that express a universal idea of justice and symbolically structure the political environment. Laclau understands populism as a specific type of political discourse, a logic he attributes to the term 'the people', a protagonist position used to challenge a given power structure. Concepts such as 'the people', 'the establishment' and 'the elites' are empty signifiers that can take on different meanings depending on the speaker and the context in which they're articulated; they can be mobilised against an elite that is perceived to oppose one's well-being. Importantly, Laclau argues that populism is not a threat to democracy. Instead, he argues, it is an essential component of it and a way to revitalise politics.

In many ways Sara is testament to the way in which the rapid stops and starts of the economy over the last few years have opened up the space for new groups of people to enter the political arena and call into question the motives of those who have held power, rethinking what political structure would work in place of the previous one. This gap has, in fact, opened up the space for a new kind of subject that attends to the ethics of the self. Populism here is a concept that can be reactionary or progressive, democratic or anti-democratic, depending on the actor that incarnates it and the context in which it manifests.[4] We need to explore not just what populist rhetoric does (à la Laclau) but also explore the content of populism and examine how such worldviews have arisen in the first place.

Although populism is often viewed as born out of a critique of democracy (sometimes it may be seen as a danger to democracy and be against many of its fundamental principles), at other times it may be seen as a necessary rupture of the usual politics, when they have reached a tipping point or cease to speak for the whole people. Here populism emerges on the cusp, heralding a new way of doing politics to revitalise democratic processes and recalibrate them to the needs of the citizens they serve. This rupture emerges most prominently under conditions of economic and political crisis and especially as an outcome of austerity measures.

While forms of populism may be similar in different places, the content of populism differs widely from left to right and points between. In Mongolia populist rhetoric cuts across mainstream left and right parties and can be understood as a reaction to rapid economic policies including the hyper-financialisation of the economy with the increasing political and economic power of the banking sector and the intensification of foreign-fuelled resource extraction at the cost of growth and the well-being of local communities. Sara has seen first-hand the way that business and politics merge to benefit the few, leading to what she sees as corrupt morality.

Outward change sought through inner knowledge

In searching for a new kind of political framework that does not simply flip between one extreme and another, Sara appears to be looking outwards for possible exemplars to follow and on which to model herself (see Humphrey's [1997] work on the prevalence of exemplars as teachers in Mongolian ideas of subjectivity). At the same time, she is also practising an inward search, attending to her 'soul' as an exemplar for whom to be in the present. This kind of internal self-definition is reminiscent of what Humphrey (2008) has pointed out: 'In Mongolia everyone can assume different relationally defined kinship positions, they can also see themselves as constituted by a singular "soul" (*süns*)' (Humphrey 2008, 369).

Choosing to focus on her (ancient) soul as an exemplar for who she is in the present, Sara fixes on a new identity – an archetype and figure that grants a break with her previous (capitalist/splintered materialist) self, focusing instead on an essential singularity. This is a version of herself that she chooses to cultivate and give prominence to. When she marshals knowledge from the past as a template for how to live in the present, echoes of previous people act as templates for future forms of subjectivity, prefiguring a world she would like to live in. It is fitting that her soul is a thirteenth-century queen, since this recalls previous times of change, such as the 1990s, when Mongolians also sought exemplars from their 'deep' historical past (Humphrey 1992).

On the one hand, dressing up in costumes from the thirteenth century shows a respect for the state that emerged at that time. On the other hand, this is a time period that Mongolians often refer to when they want to seek a new model or exemplar. For example, Kaplonski (2004) notes that in the early 1990s it was common for people to re-evaluate aspects of Mongolian history previously relegated to the periphery or banned during the socialist period. This was a time when Mongolians were interested in constructing a past that established Mongolia as a distinct nation, separate from China and Russia. He explores the way in which Chinggis Khaan was a moral exemplar for the nation and for the creation (reassertion) of the Mongolian state and Mongolian independence and identity (Kaplonski 2004, 121). Kaplonski delineates three different ways in which Chinggis Khaan was venerated as exemplar in Mongolia in the 1990s; in the third strand we learn how Chinggis Khaan was seen as the progenitor of the Mongolian nation, rather than as an individual per se: 'There are a number of variations within this trend, such as the emphasis on Chinggis as administrator, law-giver or humanitarian'

(Kaplonski 2004, 131). The image of Chinggis Khaan as a skilled and innovative lawmaker and administrator is often venerated in the public imagination and marshalled as a critique of current politicians, who are criticised for not being able to 'carry' the state in the same way.

Chinggis Khaan and the apparent success of his nation-building project have become a recurring exemplar for many different articulations of Mongolian identity and nationalism. Lhamsüren states,

> The Mongols' origin and descent myth is deeply interwoven with the history of Mongolian statehood and its foundation and the then still intact ruling lineage, the Chinggisid lineage, as the Mongol chronicles of the seventeenth and later centuries testify. (Lhamsüren 2006, 67)

According to seventeenth-century chronicles, Chinggis Khaan's ancestors were the ancestors of 'the Mongols', turning a single descent group into a nation by combining a common bloodline with a mobile descent group that ruled over Mongolia. 'Furthermore, the Chinggisid lineage and nobility was the provider and constructor of the Mongolian collective identity for they inculcated and educated the Mongols with the idea of a separate Mongolia' (Lhamsüren 2006, 74). In spite of this constructed idea of unity across generations, Lhamsüren (2006) is quick to point out that what distinguishes modern nationalism from these pre-modern sentiments and loyalties is the introduction of democracy, with its idea of citizens and a community of equals. It is exactly this aspect that people like Sara and her group see as corrosive of current political life – something they would rather was eliminated.

A similar kind of logic was articulated by one of the members of our advisory board. During one of our meetings an environmental lawyer, who had represented clients that opposed mining projects, spoke of the need to find new ways of imagining state power. He reported on discussions about reviving and reinventing the ancient Mongolian system of *Aravt*, the empire-era Decimal System of Tens, as a new way to structure political life. It is reputed that Chinggis Khaan instituted the System of Tens as a military system – whereby one person in a group of ten reports back and leads the group, scaling out to 100, 1,000, 10,000, etc., building up units through a system of tens. In this way the ruling of a country is distributed into nested hierarchies without a single leader, but with multiple leaders or heads who meet through the *Ikh Huraltai* and the *Baga Huraltai*, giving rise to parliamentary meetings of aristocrats (see also Kaplonski 2004, 135).

Forms of organisation drawn from the historical past are thus taken up and promoted, by a range of different interest groups, as alternatives to the current parliamentary system. Drawn from a period of Mongolian history when the nation flourished and expanded, for people like Sara, who are in a sense part of the elite, these forms of social organisation appear to be home-grown alternatives to a colonising democracy. Amplifying ideas from Mongolia's ancient past, people like Sara mobilise them in different contexts, allowing them to cultivate themselves as subjects in the present. (On ideas about the ethical subject, see Laidlaw [2002] and Robbins [2012].)

Concluding reflections

At the risk of sounding totally functionalist, we may conclude that attending to her thirteenth-century soul-self provides Sara with a focus, a template for a new form of subjectivity that has arisen out of her current dissatisfaction with politics, her experience of being at the coalface of the property market, and in discussion with her friends, many of whom are in politics. Born out of a kind of political awakening, recourse to the thirteenth century has resonances with other more 'nationalistic' groups who marshal political critique of current politicians and foreign investors in Mongolia. Such groups look back in history for exemplary ways of being as a nation and as individuals (see Kaplonski 2004). From cultivating this version of herself, Sara's religious and metaphysical life mirrors her political reawakening, promoting a move towards forms of *self-governance and care* both for Mongolia as a nation and for people themselves.

This kind of vision stands in stark contrast to Tuyaa's life, which I turn to in the next chapter. Here we will see an existence that is held in place across a distributed network of friends and institutions who broker favours with each other. As objects are held in pawnshops, loans remain outstanding and care is shared across a range of people, spreading risk and resources. This form of networked subjectivity is not unlike the wider economic practices we find prevalent in Mongolia, where businesses exchange favours and resources in groups that bid for wider tenders and share accounts. It is not unlike the way in which many Mongolians live from loan to loan as finances are spread across multiple spheres and never contained in one place for long (Waters 2018). It is the opposite of Sara's search for a more centred politics and focus on the cultivation of self-care. It is a way of life that involves a splintering – both physically and emotionally – and the trading of care for money.

What do these two forms of subjectivity – one singular and determined internally, the other multiple and processual, distributed across a network of people – tell us about the forms of capitalism prevalent in the gap? On a general level they point to modes of relating that appear to be diametrically opposed. One is defined by helping, holding and sharing, while the other is determined by accumulating, gathering and containing. Such a tension also points to the internal contradictions of government policy in Mongolia over the past 10 years or so. On the one hand, the government has opened up to new forms of foreign investment and debt. In fact, it was only with the mining boom that the government was emboldened to take out various forms of sovereign debt, thereby making small-scale loans available through banks, non-bank financial institutions and pawnshops. This trickle-down effect shows how the accumulation of sovereign or national debt becomes linked to personal debt – so that a nation's indebtedness to others affects its citizens. As Bear (2015; 2016) has noted for India, the rise in microfinance and small-scale loans is linked to the issuing of financialised forms of sovereign debt that boost the levels of credit within the banking system in order to extend personal debt.

At the same time, the Mongolian government has also acted in the opposite direction. Deals have been renegotiated and shares of ownership recast, prompting foreign investors to label Mongolian politicians 'nationalist', intent on initiating a 'resource curse' as the government seeks to retain the nation's wealth for future generations. Such a perspective (for both individuals and the nation) depends not on inter-subjective exchange but on an intra-subjective exchange, whereby one recognises the future as it might manifest internally. To call this simply 'nationalist' or 'populist' is to miss the complex range of things that are being kept inside and how they may be held in place. (I am being deliberately vague here in order to draw an analogy between boundaries of the nation and its subjects.) When hope is found in a version of oneself that is within the boundaries of what already exists, it is perhaps more accurate to say that it calls into being a new way of understanding what exchange might be. It also highlights a different range of assets that may be considered resources for a nation and its people and values a different understanding of profit, benefit and growth. As many look to resources from the 'deep past', both historical and ecological, they shift fundamental understandings of value and of what politics is. We need to look at the selves being cultivated through such practices and at the worlds being brought into being through such cultivation.

Notes

1. The Samsung Galaxy Note 7 was banned from flights because it allegedly posed a fire hazard. See: https://eu.usatoday.com/story/news/2016/10/14/dot-bans-samsung-galaxy-note-7-flights/92066322/.
2. This, it appears, is 'not how people classify [and arrange the world], but how they speculate about the universe and their place in it' (Skafish and Viveiros de Castro 2016, 397).
3. This way of articulating new political ideals is reminiscent of how politics unfolds in Mongolia. Although there is a head who leads (an *ezen*), democratic politics continues because of the existence of 'interlinked patronage networks' that disperse political power (Radchenko and Jargalsaikhan 2017, 1035). In a similar way, Sara and her husband move between different groups, creating connections, developing new theories and ideas and formulating ideas of how they would like the future to unfurl.
4. In a symposium on populism in *Economic Anthropology*, Ho examines the content of populist critique in the US. She argues that populism here 'deploys the rhetoric of reverse discrimination and scapegoating to galvanise political energy in the name of the "common man" [mainly white, male and heterosexual], within a context of intensifying socio-economic inequality' (Ho 2018, 148). Those who have benefited most from such changes are the financial elite who frame this inequality as an outcome of 'cosmopolitanism, meritocracy and multiculturalism'. Reactionary populism, such as that which led to the election of President Trump, arose, Ho argues, out of real grievances against these neoliberal forms of financialisation. However, it is unsound to conflate policies and practices that benefit the financial elite with the demands of marginalised and minoritised groups. Given the way in which narratives have been interpreted and reinterpreted and forms of explanation appear multiple and contradictory, Ho calls for 'a critical form of economic anthropology' (Ho 2018, 149). Such an anthropology would explore the social construction of particular markets that have created particular worldviews, sensibilities and prospects for many Americans. It would work to uncover and destabilise certain financial myths that have held the economy in place in a very particular way, mostly for the benefit of institutionally privileged white men. What she calls the burden and continual challenge of economic anthropology is to unpack these resentments and illuminate their relation to the financialisation of the US and global social economy in general.

Interlude II

Zorig is a 32-year-old father of two. He met his wife while they were university students, his university fees having been funded by the hard work of his parents. They live in a small flat near the main outdoor market in Ulaanbaatar. As a youth of 14, Zorig grew up in the countryside and learnt to gather pine nuts with his brothers in the forests that surround his parents' winter encampment. They would set off in the autumn on horseback with their dogs, heading into the mountains bordering Russia for several weeks at a time. Before this he had spent his summer holidays looking after the cattle and fishing in local rivers. His school days in the district centre – living with his eldest brother and sister-in-law – started and ended with collecting water from the neighbour's well and preparing firewood for the day, chores I used to witness and help with when I lived with him over 20 years ago.

After finishing university Zorig worked at a construction company, and then for some time he helped his older brother build wooden cabins that they sold to people in the city. One of these large jobs remains outstanding and they still haven't been paid for over a year. In 2011 he worked for a company in the Gobi Desert, helping to erect the electrical power station for the Energy Resources coal mine. As contracted workers, he and his colleagues lived in a ger camp and were fed all meals on site. Every 11 days they were paid MNT800,000, but some were paid even more. This was a time of plenty, both in the visions that flourished for the future of the country and economically. Despite the salary and stable work, Zorig hated the location. As he came from the Hangai forests of northern Mongolia, the Gobi was unbearably hot and dusty. There was little water, and that which was available from wells tasted bad.

When the construction company he was working for relocated to the other side of the city, he was unable to make the long commute each day and lost his job. After searching for some time, he was finally able to secure work in a nearby sewing factory. Lit by strip lighting, the factory has no windows and the air is dusty. To counteract the noise from the machines, workers wear small plastic earplugs, but the sound is still deafening. Unable to sew the bags himself, Zorig was allocated the manual task of working at a machine that bound the sacks into large piles of 50 or so each. The machinery he worked at shook vigorously. After only a few months he began to feel the impact of this monotonous work on his body and developed acute backache. The impact on his back was so painful that he was unable to get up for several weeks.

Returning to work, he was allocated a new job sewing large sacks at a sewing machine. At first his output was very meagre. He had to learn to sew through his mistakes and was paid according to the number of sacks he could sew within an hour. He hopes that in time he will increase his speed and be able to earn more money. The bags made in his factory are large white hessian sacks with black writing printed on the front announcing boldly,

PRODUCT OF MONGOLIA

In the autumn of 2016 I am able to visit the southern Gobi Desert for a second time. It is here that I notice Zorig's work being put to use. These bags are used to transport raw materials directly from the mines in Mongolia to China. When you see them here, there is a sense of pride in their proclamation 'PRODUCT OF MONGOLIA'. But seeing them transported immediately from the mine to the border adds a sense of desperation. This national display of ownership is a hugely important but short-lived spectacle with very few observers.

At Mongolia's largest gold and copper mine, Oyu Tolgoi, Mongolian workers work long shifts to extract minerals that are 34 per cent owned by the Mongolian state. This hard-won portion of ownership does not generate any revenue (it only pays back loans) and the nation will not receive an income from this mine for another 20 or more years. Entering the site, one gets the sense that it is its own country with its own rules, separate from the landscape in which it sits. This atmosphere is only slightly splintered when one goes into the mine's canteen – a large social space full of people sitting at long tables eating their lunch. On closer inspection one notices slight differences among the people sitting there. On the backs of their coats are the company names identifying different contractual teams working on different areas in the mine. Not completely one unified corporation, then, but a conglomerate; a collection of contracted companies working in one place.

There are further paradoxes. Witnessing how copper concentrate is being mined, produced and bagged in Mongolia (as a 'product of Mongolia', no less), it is strange to see how this product is then driven straight out of the country to China, only a few kilometres away. In fact, the whole mine is powered by electricity bought from China and the only one to gain any profit from this raw extraction is the foreign shareholder of the mine.

Just before these trucks reach the border, the road merges with another one – smaller and narrower and much more dangerous – that provides the route for thousands of 100-ton coal trucks from coal mines slightly further west. This road forms a large loop on which truck drivers may spend as long as three months at a time, making the journey from the mines to the border and into China to dispose of the coal at large stockpiles, in return for payments in Chinese yuan. Mongolian drivers are driving Chinese trucks owned by Chinese companies containing Mongolian coal along roads that have not been turned into railways, in order to bring coal to the border to pay off debts owed by Mongolian coal companies to Chinese ones, to which they are locked into contract prices below market value.

Following the copper concentrate and coal down to the Chinese border, you pass by the world of truck drivers, displaced herders and disgruntled community leaders, small-scale illegal rice and scrap metal traders, yuan money changers, border police and prostitutes, in what some optimistically call 'Mongolian Korea', where cash seems to fall into the hands of some in return for hard labour. My mind casts back to Zorig working in the sewing factory with his aching back, struggling to make enough money to feed his family, but proud too of his contribution to a Mongolian industry. The mining industry brings a strange collection of people together, opening opportunities across a range of different spheres, and closing others.

Here the world feels locked into a kind of castrated sovereignty, where some seem to be benefiting while others are locked out from profit. Perhaps this is the raw frontier of the contradictions of capitalism, where multiple stakes and claims to ownership cast people's lives in seemingly absurd ways. The mine brings together splintered groups of people that enable it to exist. Locked securely into global trade agreements and loans, the larger corporations that own this place seem exempt from any kind of greater accountability. Instead, a temporary opening is forged, in the landscape and in time, where they momentarily benefit from the extraction of these natural resources for an unknown period.

Figure 3 'Fire' *Gal*, by Nomin Bold, 2016. Acrylic, canvas 245 × 145 cm.

3
Loans for care

This chapter outlines some of the individual ethical projects of those living at the urban margins of Ulaanbaatar, Mongolia's capital. It focuses on intergenerational forms of care that take hold when state care is increasingly absent, withdrawn or inaccessible, and highlights the economic component of this care. It also looks at issues of debt, secrecy and shame as residents harbour mistrust and fear of each other and of the state. In focusing on these issues, I will explore three generations of one family. Through them we see the way in which care becomes synonymous with money as people are entangled in different levels of debt. A mother grants care to her only son by financing his education. In turn she receives money as a form of care from her co-workers, who grant her informal loans for her medical treatments. Her mother, in turn, gives up her state-awarded pension in return for the care her children grant her in old age. In each of these cases elements of economic strategising, decision-making and calculation within kinship and friendship networks come into play as people are co-dependent on each other for survival. While facilitating certain livelihoods, these elements also come to hold people in particular ways, creating temporalities of flows, stoppages and constraints.

*

In many ways it is easy to characterise the lives of the people in this chapter as occupying the 'suffering slot' (Robbins 2013),[1] that is, as subjects who, in the context of deregulation and the retreat of the state, are left to fend for themselves. Living in 'zones of abandonment', these 'suffering subjects', to use Robbins's (2013) term, experience the universality of trauma, thereby promoting widely accepted models of the good. Robbins argues that anthropologists need to resist such assumptions and descriptions and 'document the different ways people live for the good and find ways to let their efforts inform our own' (Robbins 2013).

In working closely through the ethnography underpinning this chapter, I have come to recognise that much of the economic and emotional work that people engage in is not just an outcome of things imposed from above or outside, but can be viewed as a kind of 'ethical calculus' that is taken up as a strategy by individuals themselves.[2] This involves taking economic risks while hedging one's bets – sometimes with people one knows and has long-term relationships with, and sometimes taking a risk as events present themselves. The impetus for such work, which is emotionally and financially taxing, is that, ultimately, it amounts to a form of care for those who come under the umbrella of your household and for whom you are responsible. An 'ethical calculus' amounts to a technique or strategy by which people strive to achieve a better world for themselves and those they love. Different from the philosophical term with the same name that uses mathematics to compute ethical problems, the term here is used more in line with the feminist concept of 'mental load'. It is motivated not by profit in a monetary sense, but by the impetus to care for the needs of others and oneself.

Thus, I see the lives of the people I shall describe in this chapter as driven not so much by what they are *subjected to*, which may be similar to the experience of marginal urban populations elsewhere (see Han 2012), as by the subjectivities they carve out *for themselves* in a world of very particular kinds of constraints. This follows Zigon's (2014) critique of the 'ordinary ethics approach' – namely, that the study of ethics is not really about the judgements we arrive at when we stand apart from our ordinary practices. Instead of assuming we know what the language of morality and ethics consists of, I focus on the way people *act 'ethically'* in worlds that seem to have forgotten them. Following Zigon (2014, 759), we see how people create an 'ethics of dwelling', 'of being', and in so doing are engaged in a 'politics of world-building'. This involves creating relationships that recognise their needs and carve out a space for care. This is not a world that necessarily pre-exists within language, but one that has had to be made anew by the people I describe.

In this back and forth between hopeful opportunity and constrained present, the people's lives resonate very much with that form of subjectivity defined by Evans and Reid (2014) which I touched on briefly in Chapter 1 as characteristic of late capitalism and determined by the state increasingly calling on its citizens to be 'resilient' (see Chapter 1). Reid (2012) argues that whereas liberal democracies around the world used to focus on offering their subjects security (health, welfare, business, environmental, political and economic) – something that has been changing with the realisation of climate change, ecological collapse and wider shifts in the global economy – they are now demanding that subjects learn to be resilient. He states, 'Building a neoliberal subject involves the deliberate disabling of the aspirations to security that peoples otherwise nurture and replacing them with a belief in the need to become resilient' (Reid 2012, 149).

When the very idea of security is disabled, danger is not always something to be avoided. Instead it is something we must learn to 'live in exposure to'. Reid argues that we are increasingly required to 'live out a life of permanent exposure to dangers that are not only beyond [our] abilities to overcome but necessary for the prosperity of [our] life and well-being' (Reid 2012, 145). In this sense, capacities for resilience involve at once securing yourself from danger (biological, environmental, financial) while at the same time exposing yourself to forms of danger and risk that allow you to benefit. This capacity is what Reid refers to as 'bounce-back-ability' from an ordeal or event: turning fragility into wealth, weakness into strength. Resilience, he argues, is characteristic of neoliberal forms of subjectivity and 'is the human art of living dangerously'.

This focus on the way in which communities are required to be resilient echoes similar studies of those who live on the margins of the state in late industrial capitalism (see, for example, Han 2012; Fortun 2014; Biehl 2005). These works often highlight that, though everyone is called on to become more resilient during times of austerity and cutbacks, the people who are the main targets are those populations most vulnerable to global and economic change (i.e. they are different people from those responsible for creating the conditions that produce their vulnerability).

Given this broader definition, one may ask what happens to communities of people when they are required to be resilient. Do they retreat into their own families and collectives, or do they reach out and form broader communities of care that take the place of state support? Ethnography elsewhere has confirmed the way in which networks of care do not just internalise but reach out and take the place of that once offered by the state (Garcia 2010; Han 2012; Yang 2013). Such forms of care are also a feature of current forms of neoliberal capitalism in Mongolia's ger districts. Here the retreat of state support (or its continual delay) has led to informal lending and individual debt. As short-term individual debts accumulate, ways of life are constantly rendered precarious and temporary, requiring subjects to be resilient and to bounce back from adversity in diverse ways while caring for those who facilitate their existence. In this context, I will argue, paying attention to an 'ethical calculus' allows you to leverage yourself and bring the needs of those you care for along with you.

As we saw in Chapter 1, Oyunaa had to relearn how to live in a context where multiple outcomes have to be accepted as possible, since a singular path that one can bank on is not always possible. In this chapter, we see security further destabilsed, to maximise possible outcomes for those in your care, but a secure dwelling is also sought. The following will reveal the way in which people navigate the state's demand for people to be resilient and bounce back from exposure to insecurity (especially through the encouragement of debt as a necessary danger in the pursuit of prosperity), and the intimate practices of care and place-making (or dwelling) that people work hard at for their households.

Tuyaa and her family

Tuyaa is a 49-year-old unmarried woman with a 16-year-old son. They live together with her almost completely blind mother in the far eastern part of Ulaanbaatar's sprawling ger district. She has to be a mother, a daughter and the head of their household. She works full-time at a state nursery in the outskirts of Ulaanbaatar, in an area known as the ger districts, where people live on plots of fenced land in Mongolian felt tents or wooden structures that are mostly made up of one room.[3] Working parents leave their children at her nursery in the morning around 7.30 or 8.00 a.m. and sometimes don't return until 10.00 p.m. In the winter there is no outside space and the children, aged between four and six, are forced to play indoors in groups of up to 45. Strict nap times and toilet visits are enforced, and food is cooked on site. After this very arduous job, Tuyaa walks home and cooks, cleans and catches up with her mother, who never leaves the yard they live in.[4]

In the spring and autumn of 2016, I spent several weekends with Tuyaa and her family. Taking the bus to the outskirts of the city (it only goes as far as a residential area known as *offitsyer*), I waited for enough people to gather to take a shared informal taxi to her area and then walked off the main road up various smaller roads to her yard. That car ride cost MNT1000 in addition to the MNT500 for the bus. Although the family were located fairly near to the city centre, they visited it rarely. I often bought gifts and basic food at the small shop on the roadside. Visiting Tuyaa, I came to realise that her life existed on a tight shoestring, something she balanced with great care and attention.

Recently, however, this balance had almost fallen apart, for she was diagnosed with a cancerous tumour and had to have her womb removed. The operation was carried out in a hospital in a provincial centre (because it was cheaper than in the city) and she only stayed for the minimum number of days in order to save money. Resilient to the point of causing potential harm to herself, she was desperately trying to keep things together. However, in spite of her health, and the death of her sister a few months earlier, she planned to return to work, which she had only recently started, in a few weeks' time to resume her duties. This would allow her to make sure that she had the necessary sequence of state stamps in her social insurance book to qualify for a national pension and that she had the funds necessary for her son to graduate that summer.[5]

Following Tuyaa, we learn about the pressures of intergenerational forms of care that take hold when state care is absent or inaccessible. We learn of the movement of people from the countryside to the city and the importance of family and extended networks. We shall also see the individual ethical projects of those living at the urban margins of Mongolia's capital, where issues of secrecy and shame prevail as residents harbour mistrust and fear of each other and the state.

In and out of place

'Hey! Hello! What's your name?' shouts Dulam across the fence that divides her yard from her neighbour's.

'Bold,' a man's voice calls out flatly. 'My name is Bold,' he adds, before slamming the door to the outhouse and walking away.

This is the extent to which Dulam, Tuyaa's elderly blind mother, knows her neighbours. Tuyaa knows some of the local children through her work at the nursery, but apart from the people living in their yard (hashaa) that's all.

Now almost completely blind, Dulam spends her days confined in this fenced enclosure. She lives, sleeps and eats here and hasn't ventured out of it since the truck delivered her two years ago from her home in the countryside. She had arrived against her will, after the death of her husband, pressured by her family to stay with her youngest daughter in the city. She suffered from car sickness and had to be carried from the car after 18 hours of non-stop vomiting.

In Ulaanbaatar it is currently −22°C. Dulam cannot light the fire by herself, so her daughter stokes it up in the morning and hopes her mother can add a few pieces of coal or wood throughout the day. One time, Dulam recalls, she heard a rattling at the fence and went out to see who it was. Whoever it was did not answer her calls. All she heard was the slamming of a door and a truck speeding off. Possibly someone chancing their luck to see if the enclosure was empty, she thinks. It is lonely, she concedes, and during the day she craves visitors.

Tuyaa works to fund her son's impending university education and pay off her multiple debts. She is also collecting state stamps in her social security book (*niigmiin daatgalyn devter*) in order to qualify for a pension in a few years.[6] Her mother's pension is now completely non-existent, having been collateralised so that bank loans can be taken out against it for several years to fund her grandchildren's education and the medical care that allowed her now deceased daughter to be taken abroad for treatment. A past financial resource, she is now mostly a financial burden.

Even though she has lived here for several years, Tuyaa does not own this plot of land. It belongs to her sister's husband, who lives in a larger house on the plot with his family. For three years Tuyaa lived in a leaking and cold felt tent with her mother and son. Last spring she pawned all her jewellery, including her earrings and a necklace, to a local pawnshop for an 8 per cent cash advance for six months to hire a truck and pay men to take down her small one-room wooden house and transport it from the countryside to be erected here (for a similar example see Fox [2019, 110]). They arrived at night and put it together quickly. This is something she laments as I enter with her for the first time: she complains that it was not done properly.

Tuyaa and I first got to know each other 20 years ago in the small village where I carried out my PhD fieldwork. (I use the terms 'village' and 'district centre' interchangeably, although the later is a more direct translation of the Mongolian term *sumyn tövd*.) As the postal lady who managed the only telephone line, she knew everyone's news and was the absolute centre of people's lives. She brokered favours, passed on information and packages and sent on messages scrawled in neatly folded little handmade paper envelopes. She was upbeat and fun and always had a joke to share. She was only 18 when she started work at the postal office, and she held the position for longer than anyone else. People from all over the province recognised her voice; recently, while she was in hospital in the provincial capital, two people across from her bed recognised her voice and asked if she was the postal lady from the village. She talks very warmly about this time, mimicking the voice she used to put on and joking that she knew everyone's business. She left the post office, which is a government institution with government-appointed employees, because of the party change when the Democratic Party came into power in 2003; she had been a staunch Revolutionary Party supporter all her life. I had spent many afternoons sitting with her in the office listening to her stories and watching as she interacted with people. It was the perfect place for a young, female anthropologist too shy to go and visit people and ask questions about predetermined topics and the wrong gender to sit about with men drinking.

Tuyaa's parents were well-respected Buriad elders who worked hard in the cooperative during the socialist period. She was their youngest child. When she was 34 she had a son with an unknown (or known unknown) man and she remained in her parents house with her son. Her mother and I had a long-standing joke that framed our relationship. When I first arrived in the village the local community leader tried to broker with her parents that I stay in the small wooden summer house located in their yard. Although welcoming, she had been very flustered at the thought of hosting a foreign person for such an indefinite period of time and had tried to dissuade me. In the end I did go elsewhere, but she always took the opportunity afterward to poke fun and suggest that I was still annoyed with her about her decision.

When I visited the village in the autumn of 2015, her neighbour Natsag told me, while forcing a torn bit of paper with their mobile number into my hand, that it was really important for me to visit her and her family in Ulaanbaatar. Later I came to realise that this was, in itself, an important act of care. It was a way to look out for them, even though Natsag could not do so physically herself – creating and maintaining connections not for any specific return, but because she was worried about them.

When Tuyaa moved to Ulaanbaatar seven years ago she first took an accountancy course, but she could not find a job because, she commented, she was 'too old, too short and too fat'. She retrained as a kindergarten teacher and got a job, first at another kindergarten, and then at a newly built state-run kindergarten close to her house. She has to work for another seven years before she can get a pension. Her son wants to live in an apartment: he is aspirational and constantly dissatisfied with what his mother provides. She wants her son to 'go to a good school, to graduate well and go to university'.

It was clear that they had moved away from a society very much based on the economy of favours (in the countryside) and were now reliant on state institutions – pensions and formal forms of credit. Care, here, equalled money as it trickled from a mother to her daughter and from a daughter to her son. In recognising this each of them seemed to invest in reciprocal forms of care for the future: Tuyaa looked after her mother, and in return her son would look after her in a chain of dependence that anticipated future care/money. (Interestingly, the Mongolian term for 'son', *hüü*, also means 'interest' and 'investment'.)[7]

But people in the village where I did my PhD fieldwork were worried about them. When they handed me Tuyaa's number on a scrap of paper, I felt the concern of people from the countryside about those who have migrated to the city, something highlighted by Fox (2019, 31–33, 116), who argues that it is hard to define the ger district from within because it is made by people and things moving through it.

An ethical calculus of world-building

Whereas an informal economy of the exchange of favours colours life in the countryside, in the city Tuyaa's life was facilitated through the negotiation of complex payments and repayments and the extraction of monetary debt. Often, when I visited, there was a tension between the need to entertain and talk with her mother and more private intimate chats with Tuyaa about her financial situation and ambitions for the future. It quickly became clear that certain topics were not to be discussed in front of others. I found, for example, that Tuyaa was not able to speak about her complex debt relations in front of her mother. Instead, she would lower her voice, or only talk when she was certain that Dulam was asleep on the sofa in the corner, a reflection perhaps of not wanting to worry her mother about her complex financial arrangements.

Then, as her eyes surveyed the items inside their one-room building, she would talk about them as if to remind herself of their existence:

> I borrowed money from someone at the kindergarten for this bed. I paid her back, or I have almost done so, but then I needed money to pay for the surgery. The payment is in two instalments. This TV I got through a repayment scheme. I will pay it by borrowing the money from someone else, as usual. Now there are tuition fees to pay for my son, and also his graduation ceremony. We used to have some livestock, but we left it with a family to look after and now it's all gone. If only we had sold them we would have made some money and would be living in an apartment by now.

Going on to explain that they were thinking of selling her plot of land in the district centre, Tuyaa would then quickly ruminate that they would not, in fact, be able to sell it for money; no one has any cash in the countryside, and they don't want to be paid with animals because they have no way of transporting them to the city.

Articulating financial situations like this is an important way in which household calculations are made and remade (i.e. the economy is made through the language in which it is spoken and re-spoken). They factor in different aspects of the current economy that statistics and reports often leave out. As Fox's work in the ger districts has shown, ways of assessing household wealth for state support do not recognise the temporary ownership of many household items, but just list them as present or not (Fox 2019, 162). Such accounting fails to consider (1) that many items are owned only temporarily through different rental schemes (such as those mentioned above) and (2) that many items may well be broken or out of use. Access to state welfare is thus determined by complex algorithms that approximate who is entitled to what, but do not actually reflect real need. A notable exception is perhaps 'Children's Money' (*hüühdiin möngö*), which is fairly easy to claim and a reminder of the state's presence even though most welfare is absent or impossible to access. In many ways this handout attempts to 'redress the eroded state–society relation by privatization [and] … smooth out political and economic "wounds" … construct[ing] an image of a benevolent, responsible government' (Yang 2013, 106–7). Momentary 'warmth' (such as this and earlier cash handouts) from the state is fleeting and often delayed or uncertain but is a reminder of the state's presence and power.

Tuyaa's commitment to keeping up her state stamps is a reflection of the trust she holds out for future reward, but the rest of her financial arrangements are based on her own informal initiatives. She recently got a loan from a friend at work in order to buy the clothes cupboard for her house. She purchased their television through a monthly repayment scheme, which requires her to pay interest. The washing machine, also purchased on a loan, which is not paid back yet, is now not working and her mother uses it as a chest for her clothes. The presence of these items in their home, rather than being an indicator of wealth, is an index that they are locked in chains of debt that they will probably never get out of, for the sake of things that are now broken or useless and can never be fixed.[8]

Such short-term loans provide forms of microfinance that, according to Hickel (2015), often end up making poverty worse. He argues that this is because most microfinance, including loans taken out through pawnshops, is used to fund consumption: 'borrowers don't generate new income that they can use to repay their loans so they end up taking out new loans to repay the old ones, wrapping themselves in layers of debt' (Hickel 2015). The only winners in this game are the lenders, most of whom charge high interest rates. Pelkmans and Umetbaeva (2018, 1051) note that microcredit schemes are 'now increasingly and negatively referred to as micro debt schemes', since they reproduce the inequalities they're supposed to overcome.

Women like Tuyaa and her mother are uprooted from previous networks of support and forced to endlessly take on debts that then have to be repaid through recourse to different favours, 'folding the financial back into the family', as Laura Bear (2015) has put it. For example, Tuyaa's mother has, in a sense, sacrificed her future life (her pension) for the present lives of her children. Now unable to offer more, she is totally dependent on them. They, in turn, are indebted to her for the money she was able to provide, but they are unable to repay this in cash. From this perspective the future is, in effect, held on pause as people live to survive the present.

In this space there is a contradiction between the high dependency people have on each other and the intense isolation they feel as they try to manage these multiple relations of indebtedness, staving off expectations and demands. A major feature of this networked debt is that it constantly raises suspicion and mistrust among people, who want to keep up good relations in order to stretch loan repayments or potentially to access future loans to pay off others. This sense of disconnect is further highlighted by the way in which people who live in the ger districts are not connected as a community; they do not know their neighbours, let alone the people down the road (see Fox 2019, 25–9, 33, 114–16). Being physically disconnected from the place where they live, but materially and financially bound to people and institutions in complex ways, creates subjects who are constantly caught across multiple relations, owing obligations, trading in favours and issuing debts.

People like Tuyaa are also, in a very important way, cultivating a means by which care is given and received among people who count each other as kin. They are ethically motivated through hard work and planning to create a better world for themselves and their loved ones. To be included in such household calculus is to know that one is being cared for and counted as part of a household. This is what Zigon (2014) calls an example of an ethics that may not have roots in Western philosophically defined ideas of ethics but is a deliberate activity of dwelling and world-building. It is the work of care. The ruminations Tuyaa shared with me about her financial arrangements were divulged at a time when she had been unable to attend to them because of her physical health and was trying to reignite momentum so that things could move forward.

As time went by things did move forward: they rambled on. Tuyaa was fastidious about everyone washing their hands as they came inside the house, so that her wound would heal without any risk of infection.

For two years, she explained, she had been bleeding, but she did not know what it was. When she finally went for a test it revealed a large cancerous growth.[9] As if to confirm this for herself, she showed me a photograph she kept on her phone of a large jar containing the growth, which the doctors had shown her after the operation – a massive yellow mound. Proof perhaps that the sacrifice was worth it. After the operation she spent a month recuperating, whereupon they took out her stitches and discharged her.

Once home, she went to a hospital in Ulaanbaatar every day to have the wound cleaned and redressed. On one of the days that I was visiting, the hospital had announced that the wound needed to be re-stitched. The daily trip to the hospital was expensive and exhausting. It involved a walk, a taxi and a bus ride, taking about 30 minutes. That day Tuyaa had asked a young boy who was sitting down in the bus if she could have his seat, but he was sleeping and she had to stand for the whole journey. To raise funds for her ongoing medication she had to pawn her jewellery. She was anxious to get better so she could start working to pay off her loans and raise the funds for her son's graduation. 'Now I need to sort out the pawnshop loans and send my son to university and get him a laptop,' she said, as if her internal thoughts were being externalised into thin air.

What can you say to someone who is so single-minded and who seems to be dying, but who is pushing ahead as if everything can be put right, even though she is walking crouched over, with an open wound and a massive empty space inside her body? There was a sense of tightened emotions, of Tuyaa trying to hold things together. The household was saturated in non-linguistic affects, moods, atmospheres and feelings: the emotional contours of life that characterise precarious times. She appeared caught indefinitely in a structural bind created by short-term loans.[10] The circle of debt that she found herself in held her. It consumed her, binding her to random people and businesses. In contrast, those within her household needed her attention and care. They needed her to make the household a place in which they could reside and grow.

Uncanny ruminations

There is a sense in which people like Tuyaa are living across a fragile surface that only precariously sustains them. Looking through old photos strewn across the bed, from a box kept inside the chest, we chat and reflect on life while intermittently going to check on the soup we're making for the evening's meal. As we sit here in her wooden house, and the sun sets on the horizon and shafts of light come through her windows, exposing the slow fall of dust, there is sense of timelessness, a sense of women living together for what seems like for ever. It is warm and caring, but it is also temporary, and it doesn't take much for emotions to be unleashed.

Tears are not far from the surface of things. Dulam keeps bursting into tears about her daughter's recent death, and about her father being killed during the period of political repression. She is also worried about Tuyaa's health. On one visit she talks in great detail to my research assistant Zayaa about Buriad clans on her mother's and father's side: the Sharaid and Khashgai. This focus on the past is only bound to the present through an anxious flitting of attention: a sense of being on the edge of things, perhaps, or a feeling that things are coming to a head.

As well as needing to work to pay off loans and fund her son's graduation and further studies, Tuyaa needs cash for her ongoing medical treatment. She needs to be well enough to return to work on 20 May, she reflects, in order to start getting the money she so desperately needs. She received a one-off payment of MNT80,000 for a month's sick leave, but this hardly covers the total cost of various small items, such as a box of painkillers, the dressing needed for her wound, or the MNT4500 for one big bag of wood and the MNT1500 for a small bag of coal. The numbers don't add up and there are always outstanding payments. Ways have to be found and money sourced out of nowhere.

Out of her window I can make out some newly built houses on the mountains in the distance. They were built for ASEM delegates near the ski resort built from government money, and they will be sold privately to make money for individuals (see Fox 2019, 181–3). Once we had eaten, and her mother had retired to bed, I knew that we would be able to talk freely about the things that kept her awake at night. So many different costs were impending, she lamented: 'we have to pay for water – it is 25 *tögrög* for 25 litres. Electricity is two or three hundred *tögrög* a month, but I share this cost with the others in the yard.' She muttered almost to herself, her eyes blank. It is as if this is the first time she's had chance to speak out loud about all she has been thinking while in hospital. Even if her mother is too old to understand much and her hearing is bad, Tuyaa needs to verbalise her thoughts, to put her calculations in order.

Listening to these mutterings and reflections, I realise that Tuyaa is perhaps expecting a financial contribution from me, but is mostly enacting her duty to perform care through such financial strategising.[11] A few minutes later she speaks again, looking into the distance:

> The wrong thing maybe that we did was that we left our animals with a relative to look after, but they claim they all died in the winter. If we had actually sold them we would have cash now, and it would have been a safety net when we needed it. Now we don't even have our own animals.

It feels like things are either in the wrong place or not in the right place – animals, wombs, money, stitches. She is trying to create a space to dwell and ruminate, but even the shelter of home is fragile and contingent. Things have to keep moving forward, payments have to be recalculated, or you get left behind. But not everything can be accounted for. As we tuck ourselves into bed on the floor one night, Tuyaa goes on to explain in a whisper that here at Hujirt Ulaan, where they live, there are two military bases nearby. 'You know, Rebecca, this used to be Sukhbaatar's practice battlefield, so it has been a military base for a long time,' she explains. 'Sometimes, at night,' she warns as she turns over and switches off the light, 'you can hear strange noises, not unlike a tank rattling past underground.' With nothing visible on the surface, she has come to believe there must be a secret underground tunnel that runs below their house. I find her comment about secret tunnels unnerving. I cannot sleep for most of the night, thinking of the underground tanks, of her cancer, of her operation and the networks of debt that tie her to others. I can hear her twisting and turning, unable to sleep either, probably because she is in so much pain. We get up at 6.00 a.m. and take photos and eat dumplings together before I leave. I am left with an uncanny sense that this family is, in many ways, extremely 'out of place', or rather in a place that is not their own, where tunnels and networks cut across and underneath them, leaving them disconnected and unable to live in the flow of favours that colour their life in the district centre.[12] These flows (gained through the economy of favours as discussed in Chapter 1), although also debts and referred to as such (i.e. *zeel*; see Chapter 5), are not *dislocating* but *emplacing*. They bind and harness people to each other in particular ways that may not always demand economic returns. Nevertheless, Tuyaa works hard in attempt to dwell in a world that seems to be dominated by unregulated flows and ruptures. Against the odds, she manages to find a place – for herself and her family – in a world that is moving in spite of her.

Financialisation of the family

Almost everyone I knew in Mongolia had some kind of informal loan. Pawnshops, banks and non-bank financial service centres (NBFS) are extremely prevalent and, despite people being easily able to access cash, everyone is in debt (see Interlude III). Stretching oneself between short-term loans is not always sustainable. The only winners in this game are the lenders, most of whom charge high interest rates, and even they are usually dependent on banks that lend them the money for premises and cash advances. Keeping people in debt through loans, 'politically docile and consumption hungry', is what Hickel (2015) terms 'the neoliberal development strategy par excellence'. Loans like this will never work, he argues, unless we address the conditions that produce poverty in the first place.

Laura Bear (2015; 2016) has made a similar argument. Repaying debt can be very difficult, both at the level of new forms of microfinance (which are often touted as a solution for poverty in countries such as India) and at a national level, in terms of sovereign debt. In her book *Navigating Austerity* she shows how forms of debt accumulated through microfinance mean that relationships within families are 'financialised' as people try to reclaim debts from people in their neighbourhoods and from within their kinship networks. In Mongolia, women increasingly take on debts from pawnshops and through networks of friends and colleagues, which then have to be repaid through family networks, 'folding the financial back into the family' (see Chapter 5).

With the mining boom in Mongolia the government was emboldened to take out various forms of sovereign debt, thereby making small-scale loans available through banks, non-bank financial institutions and pawnshops. This trickle-down effect links sovereign or national debt to personal debt: the financial decisions of a nation affect its citizens and their ability to pay back personal debts (see Bear 2015).

Conclusion

A major feature of the economic landscape in Mongolia is that the pace of economic change has often raised expectations, leading to unexpected outcomes of rapid growth and sudden decline. Ethnographic description of such phenomena, and how people are experiencing them, is often difficult to capture and analyse. Life in many places is increasingly characterised by the requirement of individuals to be resilient, enduring conditions of volatility or flux. What were once thought to be givens – such as notions of environmental and economic stability and progressive development – have been suspended and are shifting into something different.

As we've seen in this chapter, processes of financialisation, commercialisation, privatisation and global incorporation have radically transformed economic life, reconfiguring relations that define and govern ownership regimes. At both the personal and national scale, people are negotiating new financial entanglements (with banks, transnational mining companies, foreign sovereign bond holders, etc.). A prominent theme emerging at this interface is that experiences and expectations of ownership are shifting, with a turn towards more temporary forms of possession.

It is often those populations and groups who can best 'possess the temporary' – that is, be adaptable, flexible, opportunistic and resilient amidst constant change – who thrive, not just survive, in this new epoch (Empson and Bonilla 2019). Attention to the ways in which people do this raises questions of agency, inequality and difference. The brokering of access to assets is fundamental to how life is lived in late capitalist environments. Tuyaa's world is characterised by the constant tending of access to different kinds of assets. Without her work, both physical and ethical, the web of possibilities that holds her family in place, albeit precariously, would fall apart.

In her book *Life in Debt*, Clara Han (2012) explores how care and obligation are enacted as an outcome of the retreat of the state in Chile, requiring people to be resilient. She focuses on institutional credit as a pervasive form of finance that provides temporal and material resources for the care of kin in La Pincoya, a poor urban neighbourhood on the northern periphery of Santiago. She discusses how practices of 'self-care' and 'self-responsibility' – terms that echo themes of resilience – are advanced in health and social policy. At the same time, people are increasingly entangled in webs of debt that bind them to others through the expansion of consumer credit and an exposure to a range of consumer goods. She explores in detail how state institutions and economic precariousness are folded into people's intimate relations, commitments and aspirations.

At first glance, Han's book appears to fit neatly into what Ortner (2016) terms 'dark anthropology'. She explores 'how and when state violence is experienced as a past continuous that inhabits present life' (Han 2012, 4). In paying attention to the way people maintain connections in such conditions of economic uncertainty, Han shows 'how the dynamics of economic reforms, as well as state violence, were lived in intimate ways' (Han 2012, 17). As in other parts of the world, with the retreat of state services, and particularly state medical facilities, much care has moved from state institutions back into the home. These conditions have 'created a time for waiting', manifested in the way people's illnesses, violence and wider networks of dependence have come to shape the temporality of relations in the home. Han's work shows how life structured through debt has given rise to a host of 'immanent dependencies' among kin and neighbours. Borrowing credit cards, resources and time from neighbours and extended kin makes for *distributed forms of community care*, where debts are extended and delayed. Complex exchanges of debt and care create both a lived sense of indeterminacy and a kind of hope for a different future. They embed people in networks that maintain relations of debt, and also facilitate the appearance of a different life. In many ways Han's interlocutors appear to fit Guyer's (2007) description of an 'evacuation of the near future' as people live their lives in a kind of 'cruel optimism' (Berlant 2011) for a future yet to come.

Following the unfolding of Tuyaa's domestic relations over time, we see how the temporality of debt creates worry and insecurity. It also sparks desire and creates a striving for a new life to materialise. This tension is important because, as I've argued in the Introduction and Preface, it is all too easy to emphasise the shared precarious and uncertain aspects of life. In contrast, we may also want to 'focus on the attempts of real actors to grapple with moral dilemmas and to make ethical choices [that] can be seen as offering a positive and humane counterweight to the darkness of the work of neoliberal oppression and governmental constraint' (Ortner 2016, 60).

I feel that it is important to emphasise this tension. That is, we need to 'make room [in ethnographic descriptions] for a much wider and more diverse range of social and political projects' (Ortner 2016, 63); to acknowledge the prevalence of structural inequalities that determine people's lives, but also to attend to the world-building projects that take root within and in spite of them; to recognise that diverse visions and possibilities do flourish within the structures that make life precarious. The 'ethical calculus of care' that Tuyaa performs on a daily basis for her mother and her son, in spite of intense physical, social and economic constraints that pile up against her, is just one of the many ways that individual ethical projects continue to flourish in milieux that limit them. Here the intimate and affective worlds of people's homes act back on the places in which they are situated. In the absence of perceptible structural stability, there remains the possibility of being together in the impasse, allowing a space for rest and care as they wait.

Notes

1. In a similar way Ortner (2016) has argued that much anthropological literature on the effects of neoliberal policies has emphasised what she terms a 'dark anthropology', which privileges struggles and disadvantages in place of the 'anthropology of the good', or a focus on hopeful attempts of real actors to grapple with moral dilemmas and to make ethical choices.
2. The data that underpin this chapter comprise not only written notes but also recordings and photographs and an ongoing relationship through social media, as well as my own memories and impressions of that time.
3. It is important to note that this kind of formation is replicated all over Mongolia at province and district centres and was a feature of settlements before socialism. It is, therefore, not a new form, although its vast expansion in Ulaanbaatar and towns like Baganuur attests to new migration from the countryside to the cities.
4. My reference to it being an 'arduous job' is based on my experience of working in a kindergarten as a teaching assistant in the Mongolian countryside from 1999 to 2000.
5. This may sound jarring in relation to my description of the state's absence but is the one form of state security (along with children's money) that persists.
6. Another reason people are motivated to work without salaries is that after six months they can claim bank loans against salary stamps.
7. I thank Liz Fox (pers. comm.) for this articulation.
8. In part because they don't come with spare parts or instructions that anyone can read, since they have been made in China.
9. She explained that she had four operations on her stomach – appendix, kidney, womb and a caesarean birth – and one on her breast. When her breast was operated on, it developed a cyst and she had to rest in hospital for three months. She was 34 when she gave birth and has never been married. Her son was born as a twin but the other child died when it was born. I asked her if it was a boy or a girl and she said, 'I think it was a boy but they never told me.' Her elder sister had a child out of wedlock and then married another man. That boy was brought up by her mother as her own son. Her mother, on the other hand, gave birth to 10 children and delivered two others for their next-door neighbour.
10. This contradiction extends to the nation as a whole, chronically in debt to multiple lenders: the IMF, China, the World Bank, etc. It has no simple friends or foes.
11. I did, at a later time, give her the money for the medication she needed.
12. Here I am reminded of the call by Navaro to attend to what resonates as affect in the geographies that anthropologists study, 'breaking apart scholarly genealogies of affect that have become rather entrenched' (Navaro 2017, 210).

Interlude III

Pawnshops, banks and NBFS are prevalent all over Mongolia. You can hardly turn a corner in Ulaanbaatar without seeing signs advertising low-interest loans. Paradoxically, however, the idea that people can easily access cash obscures the fact that everyone, it seems, is in debt. Most people's pockets are predominantly filled with the anxious pressure of how to make their next repayment, and defaulting on loans is giving rise to a growing market for repossessed goods.[1]

While private debt is a shadow that looms over individuals, public debt is equally ubiquitous. In many ways the debt of individuals and that of the nation mirror each other. From 2008 to 2012 people took out large loans, banking on future growth (see Batsuuri 2015, 12). This growth has not transpired, leaving people negotiating with their debtors to restructure agreements or taking out smaller loans in order to survive.

People speculate that over 80 per cent of retirees are in debt, their pensions being a major source of collateral against which to take out loans for family members. Borrowing from those who have taken out loans, especially those with salaries, is prolific across all sectors, leading to multiple chains of indebtedness. Although Mongolian tradition values being debt free – as in the proverb 'Being rich is being debt free; being happy is being free of illness' (Batsuuri 2015, 5) – debt is now so common that it has been reconceptualised, as illustrated in the new proverb 'Money owed to lenders is not debt; it's just a loan. Debt is when we fail to pay the loan' (Batsuuri 2015, 5).

Ankara Street

Ankara Street is home to at least seven different lombards (the Mongolian Russian-derived term for 'pawnshops').[2] *The people who work here are mainly women, who brush off questions by pointing to signs pasted on walls. Their shops often nestle in the same room as hairdressers, beauty salons, restaurants and manicurists. The relationship between hairdressers and pawnshops was explained to me as being especially fruitful: as people visit the hairdressers every month or so, they are reminded to make a payment on their loan. The pawnbroker sits in a booth cut off from the rest of the room. Several cameras point at the client as they peer in to communicate, to fill out the contract or to hand over their treasured possessions in order to obtain cash. Lombard loans are easier to obtain than bank and NBFS loans, involving less paperwork and collateral, but their interest rates are the highest of all.*

Although lombards offer cash without many questions or forms, they hold on to your collateral, offset against the money given, and ask for a long list of telephone numbers of you and your family members. Pawnshop loans are not simply granted to individuals on a whim; they are a way of holding in place a relationship to a whole group of people who are all accountable for the repayment. The telephone list you hand over implicates people in a chain of debt, which is mirrored by the way the lombard owners themselves take out different kinds of loans to establish their businesses and raise the initial cash. Lombards, as one person summarised, are 'a way to get ready cash quickly', but doing so leaves a chain of people in your wake who become entangled in the circulation of cash for goods.

The shops along Ankara Street lend cash against mobile telephones, laptops, money and jewellery.[3] Interest rates and repayment policies differ slightly between the shops (between 7 and 9 per cent per month in 2015 and between 5 and 7 per cent per month in 2019), as does the amount of money they lend. They may provide different services, such as selling mobile phone units, and in others if customers take back-to-back contracts the interest rates decrease. Some lombards specialise in high-interest, quick-turnaround loans that have to be paid back in two weeks. Others, like Hiimor' Lombard, offer contracts for up to two years.

Men and women between 20 and 50 years old come here when they urgently need cash to pay bank loans, school fees, mortgages, rent or other deposits. As several people put it to me, 'young people often put in their computer to get money for a night of drinking and partying'. Reasons for accessing cash vary, but several customers explained that they preferred to be in debt to the lombard than to friends and family. 'Most lombards offer loans for up to one month for 8 per cent,' the woman who worked at Hiimor' Lombard explained. She evaluates the item to be pawned, issues a contract and receives monthly payments. Lombard workers can also be selective in whom they decide to issue a loan to:

> *If I don't like the people, I won't take their items and issue a loan. Sometimes drunk people are just sneaking around asking for money for prostitutes and drink and crime and they just bring their bad smells into here.[4]*

Unlike in European pawnshops, repossessed items are not displayed for sale in the shop. The owner sells them on to middlemen who sell them elsewhere. 'If people are not able to repay their loans,' the broker at Hiimor' Lombard explained, 'the owner sells the items to the chyenjüüd; the owner has a relationship with these people.' This fact is one of the only signs of the tarnished nature of such goods (see Højer 2012).

Observing people repaying their loans, I was struck by the stern silence of their exchanges. When I mentioned to friends that I was working on the way people access cash, some lamented that the only people doing well in the current economy must be the lombard owners. It seems to me, however, that small lombards, such as those on Ankara Street, are only just ticking over, as the chains of debt that sustain them require complex payments that bind people to each other in precarious ways. It may be because of this very precariousness – both economic and social – that the exchanges I witnessed were so formal.

Stopping and non-stop loans

Outside the city centre we find lombards specialising in the exchange of cars, garages, apartments, car parks and even plots of land for cash. As one taxi driver lamented, 'They take anything.' In the thirteenth micro-district I focused my research at a large car lombard. This consists of two sites – a large open car park with a temporary Portakabin office and a formal office where people come to make their payments.

Behind a desk in a car park sits Ganbaatar. At his side is a small safe containing car keys and behind him hangs a large oil painting of a car, on which some banknotes have been placed. People assess the value of cars with different clients outside, while one woman manages the gate.

This lombard is a conglomerate, part of the Bichil Globus Group, which includes a bank where they get their money and where all the interest rates and loans are decided. The group was established six years ago and is said to operate in many of the provincial capitals of Mongolia. It turns on a distinction between 'stopping loans' (zogsooltoi zeel, or avtomashinaa il ba dulaan zogsoold bairshuulah bolomjtoi) and 'non-stop loans' (zogsoolgüi zeel, or avtomashinaa unaad yavah bolomjtoi): between leaving your car in the pawn pound and taking out a loan, and taking out a loan and driving your car at the same time. Loans here are issued for six months at a time; any longer than this is considered too risky.

Ganbaatar is sitting in the Portakabin when a man comes in to request a one-day loan to buy a ticket to Korea. He hasn't received his salary for a few months and needs the cash today. Ganbaatar takes his car keys and ID and places them in the safe. There's an MNT22,000 admin charge for the contract, which they both sign, and Ganbaatar collects a list of telephone numbers and addresses. Some leave their cars in the pound for just one day, others for a week or even months, depending how long it takes to repay the loan. Ganbaatar says,

> It is mostly middle-aged people who come, and they are usually men. They take out loans for different kinds of reasons. If you have a car registered in Ulaanbaatar, you can access different services – so countryside people take out a non-stop loan to get cash to have their car registered here while driving it as a taxi in the city.

At the offices of the Bichil Globus Group a poster greets you, proclaiming, 'We are your Financial Wing' (Tan Sanhüügiin Jigüür), while four men in suits sit at separate desks with files and computers. One man, fiddling with a stapler while speaking on the phone, proclaims softly, 'I'm ringing you to let you know that today your loan is due. You need to make the next payment. Today you owe us 43,200 tögrög. If you come in today, we can process it.'

In this room there is a strange juxtaposition between the stillness of the office and the movement outside. While the staff phone people all day while reading spreadsheets on their computers, the company's strapline in the car park outside reads, 'Drive Your Car while Getting a Loan!' (Mashinaa Unaad Zeelee Av). A youngish man named Bold comes in to pay off MNT120,000. He goes to the till, staffed by a woman, makes his payment and is handed an invoice. The whole transaction is carried out in silence and with minimal interaction; I am not sure if this owes to a sense of shame that pervades these activities, or is simply because such transactions have become so mundane for both client and broker that there is no need for any niceties.

Bold is 22 years old and owns a Toyota IST. He recently graduated from the National University of Mongolia, where he trained as a software engineer. He put his car in the lombard five months ago and took out a six-month loan for MNT1 million. He pays MNT120,000 twice a month (i.e. MNT240,000 each month). He needed the money, he explains, for his graduation ceremony – for the clothes and so on. His father gave him the car four years ago, imagining he could make some money as a taxi driver while he was studying. He explains,

> All students with cars take out loans against them. It's a good way to get money, and my parents agreed to it. Every Mongolian has placed some of their things in a lombard to get cash. I've placed all kinds of things; a two-week loan for my phone, a one-month loan for a gold ring. The value is different according to the item. A car gets you 1 million tögrög. Now I work and am able to pay back the loan.

As it turns out, his older brother, with whom he lives, is giving him most of the money to pay back the loan. Again we see that there are no singular transactions. These kinds of exchange are always part of wider chains and obligations that reach back to implicate many different people in networks of debt. The items people use to access loans from pawnshops are not necessarily owned by singular individuals. Many of these items – phones, laptops, cars – are, in fact, held in common with others – families, siblings or friends – and are themselves 'loaned' to people in order that they themselves may access cash and take out further loans. This is a situation where very little is owned by individuals. Assets and commodities are held in a kind of temporary or collective possession and used as collateral in order to access things beyond the items themselves. Raising funds becomes a collective act, in which the extended family participates.

The stillness of the office masks the movement that the loans themselves engender, enabling different projects to be born and put into action. Behind the simple transaction of a personal possession for cash, a complex network of relations is triggered that ties people together in webs of debt, facilitating new endeavours while prohibiting others. In this domino of exchanges one thing is constant: a loan that is taken out can never be paid back without recourse to yet further loans, allowing freedom, or an opening, in one sense, while simultaneously initiating future constraints elsewhere.

Notes

1. The rate of nonperforming loans rose to 7.3 per cent in 2015. See National Statistics Office of Mongolia: http://www.nso.mn/index.php.
2. The term 'lombard' comes from a type of banking that originated in the Middle Ages in the northern Italian region of Lombardy and probably came to Mongolia during the Soviet period, when lombards were also common. Pawnshops were also prevalent during the Qing period. By the late eighteenth century, Rawski notes, pawnshops and other revenue-bearing assets had replaced grants of livestock and estates as dowry for Manchu princesses who married Outer Mongolian princes (Rawski 1998, 148–9). They were also common during the 1990s, when 'Pawning valuables became a common strategy for people thrust suddenly into the margins of poverty. The use of the *lombard* tended to become cyclical; people would surrender items as security for a loan, later, when they found the money they would pay off the debt and interest and reclaim their property, only to find that they were forced to pawn valuables again when their money ran out' (Sneath 2012, 460).
3. There is a distinction between 'material loans' (*bar'tsaat zeel*: *bar'tsaa* means 'collateral' or 'guarantee' so *bar'tsaat zeel* are loans that require collateral and *bar'tsaagüi zeel* are loans that don't require collateral) and 'immaterial loans' (*bar'tsaagüi zeel*), which may include mobile phone numbers.
4. All the lombards have CCTV cameras for protection and often hang a sheet or cloth over the safe in the back which contains the collateral, while larger items are stored off-site. The risk was based on who they decided to issue loans to. They needed to be vigilant, one woman explained, assessing correctly who is capable of repaying their loan. CCTV cameras point in multiple directions, at the hands of both the broker and the client; gathering regular repayments correctly is how the broker maintains their job.

Figure 4　'Water' *Us*, by Nomin Bold, 2016. Acrylic, canvas 245 × 145 cm.

4
Freedom and movement

On 16 July 2009 the Mongolian parliament adopted an impressive environmental law to control and limit the sites for which mining licences could be granted. 'The law with the long name', as it was colloquially known (officially, the Law on the Prohibition of Exploration and Mining in Headwaters of Rivers, Protected Water Basins Zones and Forested Areas), was intended to protect the water systems of Mongolia, on which so many depend. It allowed the government to revoke mining licences where areas were located within the boundaries of headwaters of rivers, protected water basins and forested areas.[1] Prompted by the work of civil society environmental groups, which came to be known as the 'River Movements', this law marked an unanticipated policy shift in the midst of the booming 'mineral economy' (Byambajav 2015; Dulam 2020) and provided a much-needed pause for thought at a time when everything was moving very quickly. It was seen by some as a progressive response to the 'wild' roller coaster of the Wolf Economy. While for others, especially critical foreign investors, it was an instantiation of Mongolia's ever-deepening 'resource nationalism'.

In the years that followed, however, concern grew over implementation and the government's reticence to enforce the law. Sometimes mining in areas theoretically protected by the law continued in secret, resulting in conflicts between miners and local residents, further pollution and mass protest. On 18 February 2015 (at the height of Saikhanbileg's time as prime minister) the parliament of Mongolia chose, against protest and public critique, to amend the law, which was blamed for holding back national economic growth. Amidst talk of increasing economic crisis and the halting of progress, the law with the long name was seen as having hindered Mongolia's investment environment.

This amendment allowed the government to approve the procedures for the revocation of licences granted in the headwaters of rivers,[2] and for undertaking certain measures, including the restoration of the environment in licensed areas located in the protected zones of water basins where mining operations had already commenced.[3] The Mongolian government believed that this amendment might rebuild trust between Mongolia and international mining companies, which were slowly leaving the country, and thereby boost the economy. They had no thought that what they were experiencing was the crashing wave of another global economic super-cycle; austerity and cuts – promoted by an IMF bailout – were to follow. Caught in the complex fallout of these legal amendments was Zedlen, a 55-year-old woman from Mongolia's north-eastern countryside whose work means that she sits, quite literally, at the headwater of these changes.

*

I first came to know Zedlen as the head of the local primary school in the small district where I conducted my PhD fieldwork. She had publicly chastised me for not giving free language classes at her school (instead I had offered them for free to the whole district on Saturday mornings). I thought at the time that she had been short-sighted and was surprised because she conducted social relations in a very different way from what I had learnt was acceptable in the small community where I was living. I brushed it off at the time, knowing she had suffered great personal misfortune, including domestic violence and the arson of her home. When we put together the advisory board for our ERC-funded project on changes in the Mongolian economy, however, I felt the need to diversify the group with female voices from the countryside. I knew Zedlen would be a perfect fit. When I approached her and she accepted, I was thrilled to get to know her better and find that we were more similar than I had realised.

Born in 1961, Zedlen has seen her life transformed many times. Most recently she had been working for the Ministry of Nature and Environment and Tourism as the head of the Onon River Water Basin Protected Area. When I met her in a café in Ulaanbaatar in April 2016 she was full of information about her changing work conditions. She had been through what seemed an overwhelming series of events, but, when I look back at that meeting now, certain themes emerge that make her experience familiar in the light of others I encountered. Many people were juggling job insecurity, lack of payments, insistence on continuity of stamps in their social insurance books, recourse to the law and to administrative procedures and bureaucracy, and an almost sacred attachment to documents in the face of contested claims.

In this chapter I focus on the particular instantiation of these themes in Zedlen's life. Her example is illuminating, not least because through her we learn about the precarious existence of government workers, of women and of those who dedicate their lives to protecting the environment. Her position as a state worker defending the environment is also unique in that academic work on environmental movements in Mongolia has focused on non-state-sponsored NGOs and activist organisations spearheaded by men (see Byambajav 2015; Dulam 2020). Zedlen also offers a unique insight into what she believes is the gap that her generation suffers. Through this insight we can begin to turn full circle to the gap described by Oyunaa at the start of this book.

The pressure (*daramt*): insecure jobs and shifting licences

Prompted by international environment agencies (such as WWF and the UN), in the early 2000s the Ministry of Environment and Tourism created 10 Water Basin Authorities in Mongolia to protect areas with outstanding water resources. However, by 2016 employment in these authorities had become incredibly insecure and the number of areas was reduced to five. The Onon River Water Basin Authority, of which Zedlen had been in charge, was merged with the Ulz River Water Basin Authority, which was located 330 km away. Before this change Zedlen had suffered nine months of unexpected unemployment when the government cancelled all River Water Basin Authority job contracts. During these nine months Zedlen was one of only two people (of the 17 involved) who took part in a court hearing to contest their dismissal and demand their jobs back.[4] Not long after she got her job back the protected areas were reduced and many were decommissioned. A week before I met her, Zedlen had been appointed the head of the newly merged Water Basin Authority located 630 km from the capital, in Mongolia's easternmost province. Although she was pleased to have her job back, her post had no budget apart from her own state salary, so there was very little she could actually do; she didn't even have the money to travel to the 22 districts the area covered.[5]

Many speculated that the decommissioning of this post was linked to the reissuing of mining licences and revocation of the law with the long name. During the period when the law was amended, the budget for the environmental sector was drastically reduced. For example, on 13 August 2015, during the time when the decommissioning was taking place and Zedlen lost her job, a licence was secretly granted from the Ministry of Mining and the Ministry of the Environment for mining to start at a major gold mine at the headwaters of the Onon – a project Zedlen had spent many years resisting. Corrupt and undercover dealings made the administrative structure that held things in place redundant; although she had secured a 'protected zone status' for the land extending 200 m from the riverbanks (granted by the representatives of the provincial civil office), mining could now commence. When we met, she showed me several documents and official letters that traced this process. Emboldened by her reappointment, she took a fearless stance, one that stood outside and directly challenged the networks most people worked within:

> When I next go to this mine site I will say that, since we established a protected area here, you cannot get to the river. I am intending to stand holding this document in my hand. Once the map is approved, I can hold that and say you cannot touch this – you can dig and get things out of here, but you cannot touch the river and the water.

At this point I need to highlight that the situation is complex and not simply one of corrupt national versus disenfranchised local political interests. The local government also tried to persuade Zedlen to agree to granting the licence because they were fearful that, without the company there, artisanal miners would flood the area and cause unregulated pollution, crime and disorder. The mining company has assured local people that they will only extract gold and will then transport it to a local town to be washed and processed. Some local residents have been given lavish presents and, along with local officials, have been taken to the city for dinners and offered treats by the mining company, which claims to be working in their best interests. Zedlen herself has been offered money by the company, to make up for the lack of funds in the state budget to carry out assessment work.

Crucially, however, once the licence was agreed upon, the mining company did not begin mining, but, perhaps owing to the economic downturn, they deployed a security team to protect the area from small-scale artisanal miners.[6] The situation is thus one of deadlock, of activity in lieu of other activity, and of holding things in place. This indefinite pause generates the space for speculation about motives and alliances and is characteristic of the opaque nature of politics in Mongolia (see Interlude II).

The week before our meeting Zedlen had travelled to the district of her new headquarters, where the local governor had greeted her with complete disregard: 'I have heard that the new head of this authority is very contentious and always making arguments. For how long do you intend to work here?' As I came to learn, her work encountered difficulties at every turn, with people in the Ministry, with local administrators and herders and with the people she employed, who, an audit revealed, channelled some resources to themselves.

> Therefore, because of all these pressures, I feel like I want to leave and quit my job … I am like a baby otter squeezed between rocks [*hadand havchuulagdsan haliuny zulzaga*]. I have so much pressure [*daramt*] but I need to be patient and stick with it, at least until November when I can claim my retirement. People say I should just take the money, grant the full permission to the mine and take a share. Instead I endure all these pressures, but it is hard because I am no one to the state, like a little mouse trying her best [*Töriin tölöö ogotno booj üheh*, literally 'A mouse hangs herself for the sake of the state'].[7]

Zedlen's work sits between the state and local forms of direct action. She also stands perpendicular to a local activist and NGO group that is trying to mobilise resistance against mining on specific terms, especially since the change to the law with the long name which means mining can now take place 200 m away from water sources and rivers, rather than 500 m. A group of local people from the subsection (the smallest Mongolian administrative unit) of the district closest to the river formed a political organisation several years ago and registered as an NGO to protect the area (*Goloo Hamgaalah Hödölgöön*).[8] They are not necessarily anti-mining, but they want to make sure local people receive benefits from any company profits and that the surrounding environment is not damaged, so they can continue to live there. Dolgor, a local activist and part of this group, works with local shamans to protest against mining in the area. They are extremely active both locally and in the capital, where they have linked up with the local Homeland Association and NGOs protesting against mining elsewhere in Mongolia (see Dulam [2018b] for historical detail of such movements in Mongolia). The shamans regularly hold rituals in the local mountains, ensuring the area is known as a 'sacred landscape' (see Byambajav 2015).

Dolgor and Zedlen were emphatic rivals, coveting each other's jobs. In many respects they sounded extremely similar – self-driven, outspoken and active in their wish to see the landscape they grew up in protected. It happened that some of my closest friends in the district were great supporters of Dolgor and had extremely positive things to say about her; one woman commented that she was 'an excellent lively woman who was extremely contentious' (*sergelen mundag hüühen, ayuultai hel am yostoi saitai*). 'When things happen,' she said, 'she will not just sit quietly – she even lay down in front of one of the miners' trucks, refusing them access to the mine site.' Local people commented that Dolgor was better than Zedlen, that 'she could do more'. Along with a well-regarded and highly trained local blind shaman and his daughter, Dolgor and her allies have carried out direct action against the mine company at various times.[9] When I met the head of the NGO, based in Ulaanbaatar, he was angry with Zedlen for allowing her department to sign the mining contract, even though this took place when she was redundant and she was now trying her best to restrict the licence agreement. Rumours circulated that she worked for the artisanal miners and had 'sold' the licence to the mine and got a share of the profit, along with the local district governor who now drives a smart four-by-four. Speculation about the different putative alliances was overwhelming and prevented any form of action.

Activism in action

I meet Zedlen in the countryside as she returned from the headquarters of her new office to her previous base in the countryside. It's late and she's tired, but she holds a meeting with her team, updating them and laying out duties for the month to come. I am struck by the sense that she is an excellent leader and they feel energised by her presence.[10] The situation in the eastern province is dire, she reports; there are three working mines there, but none of them employs local people and one has been overtaken by artisanal, or 'ninja', miners, so called in Mongolian because of the green plastic pans they carry on their backs to mine gold. There are hardly any trees left in the surrounding woods, and forest fires are almost permanent. The district is awash with drunk men and women who cast curses (*hel am or haraal*). Zedlen's main task is to make sure that the mining companies sign a contract to say they will pay taxes for the amount of water they use, but it is difficult to enforce.[11]

Leaving her office, we go to find the governor of a local sub-district to confirm a meeting about water and mining tomorrow. I am surprised by the way she gets things done. While it might not seem out of place in an urban office, it is unlike the normal way of interacting in the district, especially with officials.

The sub-district governor says, 'Why didn't you tell me you were coming?'

Zedlen responds, 'I called you several times and even tried to visit your house, but you have a scary dog. When can we meet with the people in the sub-district over the weekend?'

The governor looks shocked and replies, 'I don't know.'

To which she responds, 'What does "I don't know" mean? Does it mean you will let us know later? Like when? This afternoon? Let's try calling her now.'

Whereupon the man has no choice but to call someone from his mobile. With a slightly trembling voice he says, 'I've got these people right next to me now who asked me to call you to find out if they can come tomorrow at 12 noon.'

The next morning we set off in an old Russian van that Zedlen has travelled in from eastern Mongolia. The driver is anxious. He tells us that his vehicle cannot travel up hills; it is used to the flat steppe of eastern Mongolia and may not make it to the mine site, which is at the peak of a mountain range. We drive out of the district and northwards, over the large river (via a bridge funded by the mining company), only stopping to collect a Nature Protection ranger before turning east across the pasture-land to the foothills of the Gutain Davaa mountain range.

The atmosphere in the car is one of excitement. As the landscape dashes past we glance at a sheet of paper being passed around in the car. The Ministry of Environment has listed four companies allowed to carry out mining in the protected area.[12] Zedlen assures us that she has spoken to the current minister, who has said that they can't all dig here, so there is contradictory information and suspected corruption; the minister who granted the licences must have received a bribe and is no longer in his post.

We stop briefly to observe the damage to the river running down from the mountain pass, where the mine has syphoned off water to create reservoirs for washing and cleaning.[13] Soon we are back in the Russian van, crossing our fingers that it will make it up the very narrow mountain track that leads to the base at the top. At one point the car stalls, black smoke billowing from the back. The driver pulls the handbrake, places rocks underneath the back tyres and tries again. We jolt upwards, climbing beyond the treeline where a man in camouflage can be seen crouching down holding a dog on a chain and beckoning us to move forward.

Gutain Davaa Haruulyn post

Our car comes to a halt at a small plateau. My eyes cast around to see a ger, a wooden storehouse and four ferocious dogs without ears or tails, chained up and barking. Just below, on a narrow terrace, lies a large pig with piglets. Some chickens scuttle around. There is a faint singing noise as the wind bends the tall trees. We are ushered towards the ger as a man covers the eyes of the dogs on the chains. We sit down in the back of the ger and are served hot black tea and homemade biscuits. There are maybe six men and their boss, all in camouflage fatigues, watching us from the beds on either side. The boss takes out a red notebook with the words 'Gutai Raport' (sic) on it and notes down in detail who we are, our affiliation and our time of arrival. There is the low hum of a wind generator driving a television and radio.

This is the security/protection company (*hamgalach lr hamgaalaltiin alba*) employed by the mining company to guard the area while they await permission to begin mining. Their main job is to prevent 'ninjas', a Mongolian term for unregulated individuals who mine for their own benefit, extracting what they perceive as 'their' gold. The security/protection company first came to this area in 2003, and then again in 2013 when another security company took over. The leader has only been here for one year and they have little to tell us. In fact, their work seems quiet and I later learn from local herders that they hunt wild animals most days. Zedlen hands them a copy of the new resolution that they can't use any river water. They are keen to show us three large holes in the ground near to the camp, each 50 m in diameter, which they have filled with concrete. These are the ninjas' old mines, where people discovered seams of gold the width of at least four fingers.

When there was a gap in the mining licences, and in the security firms paid to guard the place, people flooded the area. One local man went up the mountain by himself and was greatly rewarded, but another family travelling up in a car suffered an accident: the car turned over, causing their son's death and their daughter to lose a leg. Gold, everyone reflected, breeds greed; no one could hold back when they learnt what existed in these mountains (see High's [2017] description of *altny hüch* – 'the power of gold').

Sub-district herder's meeting

Descending the mountain to the pastureland below, we stop at a small wooden hut where the local herders have gathered for the meeting. Zedlen knows them as her school students and friends. She gives a brief overview of the history of the river basin area, and the recent changes in administration, and then invites me to speak briefly about our project. The generator starts and Zedlen begins her PowerPoint presentation about clean water: how important it is to drink fresh water and how underground toilets pollute water sources. 'Always dig your well up-land from your toilet,' she exhorts, and then draws on several examples relating to the lives of the people she is addressing. As the talk develops into a more technical one about mining and river pollution, the driver from eastern Mongolia is invited to talk about the environmental impact of mining in his district. The floor is then opened for questions and several people raise their hands at once. There is an intense atmosphere; people want to know what is happening with the mine.

One woman explains, 'We were pressurised into signing the current agreement. They said, "Do you want ninja miners or us? You choose, but you have to choose now." And then they said, "We won't wash the gold here; we will wash it in Baganuur," and so we all signed the letter granting permission, but now everyone is worried and other people are furious with us and we want information. What is happening?'

Zedlen looks concerned but all she can say is, 'Yes, the letter of permission to resume mining was signed by many people in this sub-district and was countersigned by the Ministry. This all happened when I was out of a job, and now I am looking into how to revoke it. I will go to Ulaanbaatar and meet with the new minister and with other River Water Basin Authority people to discuss it.

I have a feeling that the only reason people have gathered today is that they hoped they would be greeted with better news. Frustrated, a man asks, 'Why do you have so many misunderstandings in your Ministry? Why, if your Ministry gave permission, are you against it? Is there a state or not? We suffer a real lack of information here and don't know who to trust.'

People go on to discuss the benefits and drawbacks of allowing the mining licence to be issued. One woman explains, 'To be frank, we were made to choose between ninjas or the mining company, and we chose the company. Everyone says we were given gifts, etc. to vote for them. The mining company passed a list around our sub-district asking us to support them. Most of us signed it. But we now realise that this makes us responsible for the consequences, and people have even spread through Facebook that we did this, but actually we didn't have a choice. They came early in the morning, at dawn, and they brainwashed us, saying if ninjas come it will be terrible; you need to sign this now.'

During their discussion a sense of unresolved confusion haunts the room. Zedlen has not been able to give them further information. They are still in the dark about what will happen and who will be blamed for the outcome.

On environmental injustice

Witnessing this local community trying to gather information and navigate the snippets they glean is humbling. I feel their helplessness in the face of an incredibly complex situation. It seems a terrible injustice that some outsiders – perhaps foreign investors – would refer to this hesitancy to allow mining to take place in their region as a form of resource nationalism. The point of concern is not how to *keep* the resources – the gold – for themselves and it is not driven by greed or envy. These people's concern is how to carry on living in a place in the way they are used to, without it being obliterated by extraction activities. I am reminded of Dina Gilio-Whitaker (2019) saying that in situations like this mining acts as 'an environmental form of injustice',[14] robbing people of a way of inhabiting a place which recognises the interrelationship of people and the ecological environment in which they live. A herder in the area, who I interviewed some 15 years earlier, reflected, somewhat prophetically, 'We don't have fences here. Our cows and herd animals don't have computers in their heads. They may wander and feed anywhere – what is to stop them drinking from the polluted waterways and streams created by the mine?'

As has been noted by other anthropologists of the region, what constitutes the 'environment' (*baigal' orchin*, from *baih* – 'to be') is broader, ontologically, than a simple biological definition of ecology and includes the varied ways humans and non-humans inhabit a place and how these relationships come to constitute the human (see Humphrey and Sneath 1996; 1999, Humphrey and Onon 1996). Of course, forms of extraction take place all the time (see Chapter 5). People take resources from the environment and turn them into profit: antlers, berries, nuts, stones and even gold are taken and traded. But local people know *how* to take their share without damaging the environment where they live (both biologically and spiritually; according to Mongolian concepts of the environment those two things are entwined) and how to give thanks for the returns.

In contrast, stories of excess, of taking too much, of losing one's mind and being driven by greed, stand out as exceptions (although who knows what the promise of gold does).[15] It seems, then, that ownership, or perhaps proper custodianship, is what is at issue. When unregulated artisanal miners pillage gold they act quickly, escaping as soon as possible to avoid the local administration, which may try to hold them accountable, and from reprimands by the human and non-human agents of the local environment. When local people help themselves to a small share (be that of antlers, berries, nuts or even, in some cases, gold), they are, it is hoped, doing so in the same way that they help themselves to other resources in the right 'usufructuary proportion' – as custodians to 'masters' (*ezen*) rather than as 'thieves / swindlers' (*luivar*). The prevalence of this relationship across multiple scales has been explored in my previous work (Empson 2014), and I believe this sense of proportionality (of a share to a whole) can also be seen to underpin many present-day Mongolian economic transactions and relations (cf. also Chuluunbat and Empson 2018).

Many are, of course, supportive of granting a licence to a large, recognised mining company. This, they argue, is 'development' (*högjil*); it is the only way that people may be held to account. Others feel gold is a kind of curse that they would rather get rid of so that they can be left in peace. But when a large, unknown mining company comes and places seven guards and ferocious dogs on top of a mountain to keep you and others out, without any information about when things will change, resentment builds and contradictions escalate. As long as the local administration and the provincial and national government remain opaque about their purposes, local people are left to feel that their current way of life is hanging on a knife-edge. An anonymous sign has been hung at the gate to the mine site which states, quite simply, 'You can't eat money.'

Adjusting to the era of society (*tsag üyeee dagah*)

It is late when we return to the district centre. We grab something to eat at the local shop and light the fire in the Nature Protection building. The men retire next door.[16] Zedlen reflects on the life events that have brought her to this work. Born in Ulaanbaatar, she graduated from school in 1978. After this she studied for her BA in Mongolian language and literature at the National University of Mongolia. Winning straight As, she got several stipends and went straight on to a master's, graduating with a high mark. In 1993 she came to the village where her parents lived and where she'd spent all her summers. She married a local man and had three children. He was an economist by training but never worked in this profession. She worked for 16 years as a teacher at the local school, and after 12 years became the headteacher.

Her husband was an alcoholic and didn't have a job, he became more and more violent. In 2000, with the financial help of her parents, she joined her children who were studying in the capital. Offering private classes at night and working at different schools during the day, she tried to keep her children safe and in education for three or four years. After a few years, she recalls with pride, they were able to save a little money and visited a restaurant together for the first time. A few years later her parents died, and in 2010 she moved back to the countryside with the idea that she would help her sister with her parents' animals and work at the local school; but they wouldn't reappoint her. That autumn a local man ran for the provincial elections as a representative of the Green Party, and Zedlen offered to help him with his campaign. It was this man who later came to tell her about the job to run the local river protection area and encouraged her to apply. She sat five different tests before she was appointed, to the great disappointment of a local woman who had held the position before her. Now 55 years old, she will be able to retire in 10 months' time. However vaguely, the state does intervene in certain ways, regulating people's life course and determining their futures.

Although conflict, jealousy, curses and feelings of mistrust surround her, Zedlen works hard to focus on her wider sense of duty and commitment to her homeland's water. Thinking back over the different jobs she has held, I have an impression that her current position, although demanding, gives her a certain kind of freedom to move between different groups of people which she has not experienced before. As she sees it, this is a freedom born out of her passion and conviction: a sense of responsibility that hard work can make things better; something, she says, that was fostered during the socialist period and is sorely missing from younger generations.

This freedom to flourish at the margins, rather than being driven by the need to be resilient, is something that Tsing (2015) has referred to as an outcome of capitalism. On the margins of mainstream economic and political life there are openings for individuals to flourish in a way they might not in more formal positions. Moving from one countryside headquarters to another – to provincial centres, the capital and back again – Zedlen has been able to move between several registers, translating ideas and issues across scales. This is not necessarily productive in a quantifiable sense (i.e. in terms of money, or the outcomes produced), but it does allow her to sustain a kind of life that she craves. In such a way she is able to straddle the tension between holding down a job at the Ministry, which believes she is a troublemaker, and reporting back to local people, who don't believe she is fully representing them either.

At the same time, it is perhaps not entirely an outcome of current capitalist logic that she is able to flourish in this space of tensions. Mongolian women, traditionally subjected to forms of virilocal residence, are masters at finding their place outside fixed networks, in the transience of movement (Humphrey 1993; Empson 2011). No wonder, they were the main breadwinners of the early 1990s, trading between Mongolia, Russia and China (see Chapter 2). This movement gives them a mobility that amounts to a different kind of power than the networks based on place (cf. Chapter 3). As I saw several times in Zedlen's dealings with – especially male – forms of authority, unable to work within them, she refused to bow down to them. This made her unpredictable and scary to some, and an outcast to others. Perhaps there is a greater place for this kind of subject in the gap than there ever was before.

Zedlen elaborated to me her own idea of this gap:

> I attended school during socialism, but when the market economy came in the 1990s I had to adjust in a huge way. For people who were born in the 60s – we were brought up not to lie, without taking sides and so on, but this does not serve us well in today's society. Now I have no car, no accommodation – nothing, except my salary. In fact, I am rewarded with very little money. In many ways I am conflicted between the way we were educated and the unjust society we have to live in today. … People like me end up becoming the victims of today's society, not the victors … living in an honest way, all I have is these burdens or outcomes. I have no emotion because there is so much pressure on me … since there are many difficulties for people they are just eager to make money. They don't place value on protecting the environment and volunteering to do so, but I work for my passion, for what I believe in, not for the money, not to get rich. Most young people I meet have misunderstood what freedom and democracy means.

Reflecting on her self-description, I am confronted with a paradox. On the one hand, Zedlen describes her singularity and difference as a product of her generation, living with one set of values in a society that has radically changed its priorities. On the other hand, it is precisely this new society that gives her the space to advocate and fight for the values she believes in. The world she inhabits is changing rapidly; laws and alliances all seem to be on the move, yet she holds on to certain things she believes in and wants to remain the same. Women of this generation, like a Tuyaa, appear to live in a world where the ground is shifting beneath them, with no solid place for them to dwell.

Singular subjects

I am reminded of Humphrey's work on the making of individual subjects in times of rapid change or rupture. She states, 'Certain kinds of anthropological experience seem to require the conceptualisation of singular analytical subjects: individual actors who are constituted as subjects in particular circumstances' (Humphrey 2008, 357). In many ways Zedlen seems to be just such a singular person. She is beyond the known categories and moulds available to her, and yet she has become who she is in very specific times and circumstances. She has a sharpened and pervading sense of who she is.

Humphrey explores the way such singular subjects emerge through the idea of the 'decision-event': something that propels the individual into becoming who they are 'such that this idea dominates other possible ways of being and orients subsequent action' (Humphrey 2008, 374). Zedlen's rupture or shift amounts to several cumulative decision-events that mark the contours of her lifeline, as she described them in our conversations, but it also coincides with the event of the collapse of state socialism and the experience of being propelled forwards into a world that recomposed the future. This event was a creative switch, a gap, that marked and 'separate[d] off times, the time of Before and the time After' (Humphrey 2008, 374). Zedlen appears to consciously live out the contradictions and the meetings of these times in her own way of inhabiting the present. Singular, yet multiple and fractured, in her continual movement and reinvention she is the gap, bridging perspectives from the past with ways of being in the present.

This movement brings to mind Deleuze's concept of the 'fold'. As a process of subjectification, the idea of the fold allows him to think about the production of subjectivity beyond accounts that presume a simple internality and externality. For the fold, the inside is nothing more than a fold of the outside (a fractal or self-scaling reciprocity of perspectives) which replicates across scales. It is a kind of mastery of oneself to oneself (see Chapter 2) and can be seen as a question of ownership. It can also be extended outwards – opening the subject to that which is beyond, which is then folded back into the subject to produce new modalities of being (O'Sullivan 2012). Life is here made in between the infinite and the finite, allowing

> access to something, the void, the 'ground', from which these worlds, these subjects have emerged. An unfolding then as that which always accompanies the fold, producing new folds but also opening us out to that which is yet to be folded. (O'Sullivan 2010)

The fold appears like a decision-event or the gap. It is a space that productively draws in from outside to open us out to that which is yet to be. Although it is able to accommodate the past in the present and make it its own (a kind of vernacular historicisation of the subject), there are differences between these concepts, which don't all signify the same phenomena. The decision-event marks a moment as rupture and event. It is the starting point, or origin, from which a new kind of subject is born. Not unlike the idea of crisis explored in the Introduction, it puts a jolt into an otherwise linear idea of time and throws into relief what counts as the ordinary. Although the gap, as a concept marshalled by Oyunaa, seems in some ways to do the same, I am not sure that it contains the same idea of rupture. Durational to some degree, but also swinging back and forth in its temporal perspective, it allows the subject to look back at a series of events and revaluate them in relation to present conditions so that, in place of failure to live up to anticipated outcomes, the subject comes to recognise a new world. Perhaps this is what Zedlen has also come to recognise. Though acknowledging the dissonance between her own morality and that which seems to underpin those around her, she has also benefited from the way in which the gap opens up a space for her to advocate and fight for the values she believes in, to exercise the freedom she seeks.

Notes

1. This law is regarded as a keystone in the struggle to prevent more than 300 mining licences being granted in Mongolia's most delicate ecosystems. It has been credited with helping to reduce pollution in water systems, especially from gold mining, and resolving conflicts where communities faced displacement by mining projects. As an international precedent for making key ecological regions no-go areas for extractive industries, this legislation also meaningfully boosted Mongolia's environmental credentials. The law affected more than 1330 licences (mainly alluvial gold deposits) belonging to some 830 legal entities (see: www.lexology.com/library/detail.aspx?g=924fef95-7ef5-4e1a-81f2-dcc5f8387112).
2. Crucially, it reduced the protected zone of water reservoirs to 200 m from rivers and lakes, whereas before it had been set at 500–5000 m (pers. comm., Byambabaatar Ichinkhorloloo, 2016).
3. For further details see: www.lexology.com/library/detail.aspx?g=924fef95-7ef5-4e1a-81f2-dcc5f8387112.
4. She was, she claimed, the only one who could use a computer and travelled to and from the city frequently; therefore she acted on their behalf and even appeared on TV to campaign for them.
5. I thank Bumochir Dulam for his comment that in many ways 'her post is symbolic', i.e. the government maintains the post in order to defend themselves against critique, but central and local government do little to support it.
6. It was explained to me that inviting artisanal miners to a mine site is a pressure tactic many mining companies have used to secure formal agreements with local governments. When I met with the head of the local NGO, based in Ulaanbaatar, he explained to me how in 2009 one of the old mine directors had been sacked for doing something illegal and in revenge had sent 500 illegal artisanal miners to the site from a south-western province. The current mining company, he claimed, had used the same threat, saying, 'If you don't grant us the licence, unregulated artisanal miners will arrive.'
7. It appears that her position does carry some power, specifically to grant legal authority to the mine, but the situation was far from clear. Even if she did have this authority, it was uncertain whether permission would ever be granted.

8. Dulam has warned, 'it is important to not mistake the nationalist environmental protestors for the Western advocacy civil society NGOs. Although there is no clear boundary or difference between the two, they are certainly not the same' (Dulam 2018b, 105).

9. In a social media post, the younger female shaman can be seen following a large mining truck, instructing the drivers to repair the road damaged by their vehicle. See: www.facebook.com/100009183161419/videos/vb.100009183161419/1600207770295313/?type=2&video_source=user_video_tab.

10. Despite having no resources they are all getting stamps in their social security books so at least their pensions can be assured when they retire.

11. It is not clear if it is the tax authority's or Zedlen's responsibility to make sure water taxes due from mining companies are enforced.

12. All we have are their names: Shoroo urt (UNB) Kompani, Avian Tes, Baihan Altan Hangai and Gutain Chuluu Kompani.

13. When I first came to the district in 1999, local rumours had it that the previous governor had signed a private deal with Ochirbat, then president of Mongolia, who owned the mining company at Gutain Davaa and would fly in regularly by private helicopter to oversee it. Over the last 20 years I have many times visited this site and some of the disused mine buildings nearby. When I first visited the mine site 20 years ago the outward physical marking on the landscape was practically the same as it is now.

14. http://culturesofenergy.com/173-dina-gilio-whitaker/.

15. My mind flits back to the story of the family who made the journey up the mountain in a Jeep and were struck by misfortune on the way down. In 2005 I recorded a similar account of misfortune at the mine site from one of the nurses at the local hospital who was caring for a small group of people who had been tasked with assessing the extent of gold in the region. They had experienced hauntings and accidents. One woman admitted herself to the hospital to escape the terrifying visions that followed her.

16. Zedlen reflects that she doesn't sit and drink with men and do politics in the way that they do.

Interlude IV

I first met Bolormaa (alternative names Michid Gyalbaa, Nomt Hatan) while we were squashed next to each other in the back seat of Sara's car on our way to a 'reading group'. Also attending for the first time, she was a small woman with sensitive, darting eyes and was rather quiet and withdrawn during the meeting. Sara kept mentioning that Bolormaa was a shaman who had written many books, but I just smiled at her. They knew each other through Gerel, who has more than 300 followers (or büleg) and is believed to be the reincarnation of Zanabazar. She reveals people's thirteenth-century souls (see Chapter 2).

At the end of the evening we exchanged numbers, but I wasn't sure that I'd ever see Bolormaa again. A few weeks later she called to say that we should meet up. I found her in the corner of a stylish café in the centre of Ulaanbaatar. She had been at work at the Asian Development Bank and wore a navy suit and shawl. Her appearance seemed incongruous with what she spoke about and she didn't really stop talking for over an hour. Bolormaa trained as an engineer in Leningrad and then in finance as an economist. She also studied for two years in the US for a PhD in traffic management at Colorado University, but such studies were not to be her fate. In 2008 she returned to Mongolia because her son was sick. At that time someone took her money and she went to a shaman to 'call her money back' (möngö duudah). In doing so she entered the path to become a shaman. Now she works during the day and writes her shamanic books by night. I call them shamanic books, but they are, in fact, an outcome of a trance-like state that takes her through nights of automatic writing which she claims originate from the Khaan of the Skies to Attila the Hun. Being from the 'Golden Lineage', with shamans on both her mother's and father's side, she has been able to reach the highest levels of the Heavenly Sky (Tenger).

Through these books, I show to others about past history, allowing people to realise that our current lifestyle is wrong. Everyone has a unique gift (bilig uhaan) and we need to make this rise in people ... The apocalypse is very close and the spirits are coming to tell us how to change things. There is a moral crisis, an environmental crisis and an economic crisis – this is a sign of this wider crisis. ... Now a new era is emerging, and everything is awakening. The person who will lead us has already been born. For us the changes may be shocking, but for spirits they don't see it as lasting for a long time and they see a new awakening coming.

Listening to her talk, I wondered how she balanced the different universes she inhabited. 'I need the money so I work at the bank, but I also need to tend to the other side,' she explained. 'Sometimes I am up until 3 or 4 a.m.' And then she was off again, describing how 'everything is fractal' (büh yum fractal), repetitive and cyclical: 'We need this knowledge to build a new world. The time has come. By 2050 the centre of the world will be in Mongolia.'

The next morning at 8.30 a.m. I attend my 'aura cleansing ritual', again directed by a woman, but this time located on the sixth floor of an office block with mostly empty offices. After my initial reading, using electronic nodes on my fingertips, I am put on a strict two-week cleansing ritual to restore my aura to its original, rounded 'egg-like' shape. Lying down on my mat, encircled by candles and ready to read my mantras, I am surrounded by men and women performing the same ritual. Posters on the walls depict Russian women and men engaged in similar activities. On a table in the corner our wallets lie in a circle next to the appropriate shiny electronic boxes containing soundscapes from outer space or Siberian birch forests – recalibrating them to beckon fortune.

This is the personal care needed to survive the precarious stops and starts of life that have become the ordinary. It is a snapshot of the silent rituals people have created for themselves to anchor some sense of stability, tying themselves to their masts as they navigate stormy waters. But it is also a glimpse of the heterogeneous subjects that flourish in the gap, the singular experiences that have given rise to people who have found a space for themselves in among the flux and transition and the paths they have been able to carve out for themselves, even when futures have not been realised as they were imagined. It is to notice the daily rituals and routines, not unlike those attended to by Saruul (see p. 18), that allow people to navigate the unexpected and emerge grounded in the present, creating a space for themselves within it.

Many of these practices appeared like fads, things that would last for a few years and then disappear again. I had to relearn what preoccupied my friends every few years or so as things changed. What was important was not so much to question the content of these things and their efficacy, but to take part; to engage in shared forms of self-care with others. In doing so, one set oneself out as part of a group of people who shared in a single vision. In this way, and here I draw inspiration from insights in Melanesian ethnography (see Leach 2002), the social relations produced out of these activities, the kind of person or subject you were making yourself into by doing them, were more important than the physical outcome of the thing you produced or performed. Furthermore, this could be a singular subject who stood out in particular ways from the other people engaged in the activity, or it could be a subject who was part of a group, network or household. The participants both showed a collective commitment to making changes and provided exemplary behaviour for others to follow suit.

Figure 5 'Wood' *Mod*, by Nomin Bold, 2016. Acrylic, canvas 245 × 145 cm.

5
Networks of exchange

This chapter opens with Delgermaa, a woman who lives as a herder with her extended family in the countryside. They have been herders for several years but have always supplemented their subsistence with other activities, many of which have been initiated by Delgermaa and for which she has received various medals and awards.[1] One of the reasons she has been so good at initiating these projects, apart from being extremely hard-working, is her ability to draw people into them. Although the profits are small and the economy in which they exist is extremely fragile and uncertain, the social relations that bind the various exchanges together are strong.

It feels important to present Delgermaa's story, for many reasons. First, it is common for city residents in Mongolia, particularly of the younger generation, to uphold a somewhat romantic view of countryside herders as self-sufficient and the carriers of 'tradition'. Countryside residents who migrate to the city, in their view, are unused to varied economic activities and at the mercy of capitalist imperatives. The reality, however, is that many countryside herders (a) started herding as a form of subsistence in the 1990s when they lost their previous jobs, and (b) have family members who supplement their livelihood with other forms of subsistence, be that trading in cashmere, informal gold mining or other kinds of 'salvage accumulation' (Tsing 2015) that bring in cash to enable the payment of university fees or the purchase of apartments, plots of land, televisions, washing machines, cars and so on. These diverse economic activities draw attention to the variegated economic landscape beyond cities. They *are* 'the economy' – their activities are not peripheral. They create worlds and shape how 'capitalism' and 'development' in Mongolia are experienced and made.

Since the 2000s the Mongolian banking sector has been liberalised and small branches of different banks have sprung up all over the country. In an attempt to inject cash into the countryside and diversify the economy, loans were made available from 2000 and herd animals were allowed as collateral. We shall see how Delgermaa's economic activities have been facilitated by such loans, but also how the economic context in which her activities can flourish – 'the market'– doesn't really exist. Debt has increased in the countryside, as in the rest of the country, through the widespread availability of bank loans. A recent change in this trajectory is that, although many people became herders because they lost their jobs during socialism, many young country people are now becoming herders as a way to pay off debts. Delgermaa's two eldest sons have returned to herding other people's animals to do just this. Rather than incentivising people to take out loans, banks are inadvertently encouraging people to become herders to pay off their debts. As Delgermaa's husband put it to me, the 'main point of herding now is to pay off bank loans'.[2]

This chapter follows a subsistence-based activity that dominated Delgermaa's household during my fieldwork, and reflects on the seasonally intense translation of common resources into commodities for sale. It looks at the subjects and relations these activities depend on and engender, including those that rely on informal or formal lending of cash or in-kind barter. We see that countryside people's experience of individual debt leads many to reflect on Mongolian political and economic life more generally, which reveals huge contrasts in wealth and outlook.

Delgermaa

Born in 1956 to ethnically Buriad parents who had moved to the area from Russia and eastern Mongolia, Delgermaa was the first in her family to graduate from tenth grade. She was then tasked with looking after her father, who had had a stroke, while her brother was in the army and her mother needed to work. On 4 August 1974, however, with four or five other people from her class, she got a job at the local sawmill. They began by helping to spread out wooden planks. Later they were allowed to work with the saw. Later still they moved on to processing.

When she was 20, in 1976, Delgermaa married her husband, Eldev-Ochir, and a year later their first son was born, followed by two more sons and then a daughter. Having three sons made her a *darhan ber*, a particularly honoured daughter-in-law, but despite this she always felt that her mother in-law judged her as inadequate. From 1980 to 1985 the family experienced some independence and moved to a neighbouring district, where Delgermaa worked in the sewing department in a Home Services Cooperative, which included shoemakers, hairdressers and photographers, and her husband worked as a woodwork teacher at the local secondary school. On returning to their homeland she worked as a cashier, a secretary and then an accountant for the local Strong Year Cooperative, calculating the salaries of drivers and others. Her husband worked as the head of the cooperative's construction and carpentry brigade. When the cooperative was dissolved in 1990 they received about 20 cattle and a pack of sacks. 'I didn't know at the time that I could have claimed more because of my position as an accountant,' Delgermaa laments.

At that moment several certainties disintegrated and they had to radically reassess their lives. They moved quickly to claim a winter pasture, where they built a small, one-room wooden house and became herders. For the first few years Eldev-Ochir herded the cattle on his own while Delgermaa stayed in the district centre so their children could attend school. After a year or so, their two elder sons joined him. When her daughter was sent to school in the capital and her youngest son could stay in the district centre with family, Delgermaa joined them in the countryside. From 1992 to 2007 they were animal herders, migrating between autumn, winter, spring and summer pasture. Working hard, they established a healthy stock of milking cattle and young bullocks, horses and mares. In 1999 I lived with them for over a year and observed how different family members come together at different pastures, according to the need for help with various seasonal activities. Their household was always a bustling hub of activity, with visitors and neighbours stopping by. Friends from the cooperative also became herders in the same area, and so, though the political landscape had changed, friendships remained.

Alongside herding animals, they were always engaged in other activities to supplement their household income. In the year 1999–2000, for example, Delgermaa sewed hundreds of winter gloves and several pairs of Buriad boots to sell in the district centre. The men of the household would disappear for weeks at a time to hunt wild animals, which they sold to city traders. In the summer months they collected berries and in the autumn they collected nuts to sell in the district centre. In 2004 Delgermaa also began to benefit from different loan schemes available from the newly relaunched and liberalised Khaan Bank in the district centre. With these loans she established a 'milk-collecting' place (*süünii tasag*) at their summer pasture, collecting milk from more than 20 households. With the help of her husband and children the milk was turned into cream and dried curds, which they sold throughout the year (see Empson 2014), and later she baked bread for sale. These activities grew until, finally, herding itself was not profitable and simply became a distraction.

In 2007 they took the unusual and drastic decision to sell their winter pasture and some of their animals and returned to the district centre, in part because her husband had become bedridden after a stroke and their sons were living elsewhere. They claimed a larger plot of land near the river and extended a one-room wooden house to accommodate their different projects, keeping several milking cattle. During this time Delgermaa worked hard (with the seasonal help of her children) to carry on collecting milk (now brought in by people from the countryside on motorbikes after the evening and morning milking) and making cream and curds to sell throughout the year, and after a year or so she established a bread-making group. She purchased a large oven and set up several different workstations, the details of which I shall go into later. These activities won her several awards and medals at both local and provincial level. It was not that she made a significant profit (her margins were tiny); it was, rather, her energy and drive that was rewarded – the way she managed to involve a large group of people in her endeavours. She was, in many ways, an exemplary entrepreneur.

Unlike Zedlen (see Chapter 4), Delgermaa has always been firmly placed in the centre of different networks. She thrives on cultivating and maintaining them. Not only have they allowed her to expand her various activities; they have also provided care and support when needed. In this she is very different from Tuyaa (see Chapter 3), who, being physically displaced, relies on state support, her salary and her mother's pension to tide her over. Delgermaa is embedded in several units of people – friends, classmates, people who shared the same pastureland, neighbours and her family – who live in relation to each other all the time, responding to each other's changing needs. From this perspective, although things change seasonally, they are also always inherently the same. Living *permanently in response to* others means adapting to other people's needs as a way of surviving, because it enables the others' support in return.[3] Perhaps it is born out of a deeper sentiment that, while places and people shift, core things remain – a kind of nomadic disposition towards social relations which implies a way of inhabiting the present in a temporary sense. This is a form of subjectivity that is continually evolving, but steadfast in its alliances and networks.[4]

The seasonal nature of various economic activities required Delgermaa to be extremely flexible, taking a chance when she could and revising decisions when necessary, as well as always working with a group of people as she continued to be located in a matrix of relations. As Pelkmans and Umetbaeva (2018) highlight for Kyrgyzstan, people like Delgermaa have to take risks all the time and can be seen as pioneers and innovators on the new capitalist frontier (for a contrasting view, see Tsing [2005] on the exploitation of nature on the frontier). After explaining her present work, I then go into detail about her previous projects and reflect on their debt and loan arrangements. This leads to a general discussion about changes in political and economic life and forms of morality, as seen from the perspective of the countryside.

Antler collection

Walking into Delgermaa's house, I lowered my head allowing my eyes to gradually adjust to the light but I was surprised to see that the floor was littered with antlers. They were contorted in different directions, with raised tines that appeared to lie uneasily on the wooden floor. I learnt later that large stag and elk antlers were also piled in the cellar outside, balanced in the beams of the attic above (where we slept), strewn across the floor in the kitchen in unruly piles, stored under the floorboards and stuffed awkwardly in plastic woven sacks by the door. There seemed to be no end to them, and more kept arriving as people returned from the surrounding forests.

In the spring of 2016 people in the district centre lamented that the economy was bad (*muu*) and that people had no money (*möngö baihgüi*). After quite a few years of small-scale loans being made available to try to diversify the economy and encourage people to start businesses, most of the projects in question had now failed and people were burdened with debt. Many resorted to herding to pay off bank loans through the rearing and sale of animals and their produce, but when the chance arose to generate money another way, usually through gathering natural resources from the surrounding forests, people seized it, because no one knew how long the opportunity would last.

It is important at this point to stress that, from the perspective of the people who live here, such 'gathering' or 'gleaning' – like the small-scale gathering of gold from the mountains (see Chapter 4) – does not necessarily contravene Mongolian notions of the protection of the environment (see Chapter 4), precisely because the people doing it are careful not to take more than their due share. If they transgress, they know they will become the victims of misfortune, something that is often discussed with local diviners and shamans (see the example in Chapter 4 of the family who suffered a car accident when driving up the mountain to gather gold) and the subject of local gossip and critique.

At Delgermaa's house, I was thrown into the centre of such an activity, which seemed to perfectly reflect the kind of capitalism that was prevalent all over Mongolia. The money to purchase the antlers collected at their house was being sent directly to Delgermaa's local bank account from a middleman in Ulaanbaatar, who also periodically sent cars to collect them. The activity was very intense, and more funds kept being transferred. Although the easy availability of antlers was a reflection of a previous three-year ban on their collection, it was suspected (*tsuurhal*, literally 'a rumour') that the flow of money from the city was a consequence of money-laundering (*möngö ugaalga*, literally 'washing money'). Delgermaa's family spoke about the possibility of there being a high-ranking person behind the scenes who needed to quickly get rid of 'dirty money' (*bohir möngö*), washing his accounts of traces of fraud or corruption, especially before the national elections. This 'cleaning' had a ripple effect outwards to the countryside, reaching the thresholds of three households in the district.[5]

The general opinion was that the city buyer (someone to whom, for 10 years or so, they had sold parts of hunted animals) was selling the antlers to someone else who would then race to the border and sell them to traders from China, where they would be ground down for medicinal consumption, and a much larger profit than the local people could ever hope for. The three local families tasked with collecting antlers were actually making a very small profit: the dirty money and the antlers were mostly just passing through them.

Although questions circulated about the morality of the men whose money they were the custodians of, people reasoned that being part of the process of 'washing' wasn't, in itself, morally bad, because it enabled the redistribution of funds that tended to accumulate in the city to local herding families who needed it. In total, 17 tonnes of antlers were to be bought from the district. Delgermaa's daughter explained that for every 150 kg collected they would be able to keep approximately MNT500,000 for their work. At this time, in the spring of 2016, one US dollar was worth MNT1990. A schoolteacher earned a salary of approximately MNT650,000–800,000 per month and so the yield was substantial. The middleman transferred money to their accounts to buy the antlers wholesale from local people. Delgermaa then took a share that they retained for themselves as their payment for the work. Calculations were further complicated by different prices for different antlers – elk, stag, white, wet, with marks (lines from a parasite or worm) or unmarked – and these were ranked according to different prices. For example:

- first-rate stag antler: buy MNT32,000 per kg / sell MNT34,000 per kg
- second-rate stag antler: buy MNT22,000 per kg / sell MNT24,000 per kg
- third-rate stag antler (with cracks and parasite marks): buy MNT9000 per kg / sell MNT12,000 per kg

One day, news came that a large car full of antlers was arriving that evening from the forests, so an advance was sought from the city buyer. The car arrived when darkness fell. The bags of antlers were weighed and assessed by candlelight in the kitchen area of the house. Delgermaa's son gave the sellers MNT7000 for 1 kg of elk antlers and MNT24,000 for 1 kg of stag antlers. It appeared to be a very large haul, one that would stand the family in some profit. In the morning, however, they found that several of the antlers were of bad quality, with lines and ridges from parasites; it was concluded that seven of the antlers that had been bought as first-rate antlers were actually third-rate. Going by weight rather than quality had put the family in serious debt, and they were worried how to make up the difference.

That afternoon, a buyer from one of the other families came round. He complained that Delgermaa's family were buying too many antlers at the highest price. All the buyers needed to be offering the same price. He quickly showed them how to fix the scales so they could make up the loss.[6] One of their sons agreed to do this, but Delgermaa and her husband commented that they didn't like tricking people. Later, they explained that they suspected the visitor might have been trying to get them to lower their buying prices so he could retain the higher buying price and be more attractive to sellers and thereby making more money.

At the same time, rumours began to spread that the main buyer from the city no longer wanted antlers. One person exclaimed that the market was flooded, but Delgermaa and her husband wondered if this was just gossip to put their family off buying more. They messaged the city buyer to ask when he would come, but all he said was that he couldn't find a car at the moment. They resolved to keep going until they had at least 250 kg more antlers. The prices decreased, but the money continued to circulate.

*

In this somewhat truncated example, I have tried to show how a seasonally dependent economic activity is prone to unpredictable stops and starts, which alter the pace of things and generate rumour and suspicion.

Chance and risk have to be weighed against future monetary debt; nothing is predictable or transparent, since prices, alliances and activities seem to fluctuate daily. 'Washing money' in one place, had the effect of creating a stockpile somewhere else – a cellar and house full of elk and stag antlers – the circulation (but not accumulation) of large amounts of cash, telephone calls to the city to try to get the buyer to collect the antlers, and mistrust among local buyers and sellers with divided loyalties and motives.

Divided loyalties, mistrust and flows of favours within networks are not so different from the corruption that local people think has fuelled the availability of money in the first place. Ruminating on political activities in the capital shed light on their own understanding of how things functioned and the way that profit was made. This activity, it is important to keep in mind, was taking place at a time when the general economy was considered to be 'in crisis'. Little or no money was circulating in the district, salaried workers hadn't been paid for some time and most commodities were bought through barter or were taken 'on loan' (chit payment). Nevertheless, seasonally intense but short-lived antler collection allowed people in the district access to cash to pay for flour, alcohol and sugar from the local shops, to buy cars and televisions, to pay university fees, to start businesses, to purchase clothes and festival foods and to pay off debts. The seasonal collection of pine nuts and berries, illegal logging, hunting for animal parts for medicinal sales, making cream and curds, collecting stones and even gold (see Chapter 4) were all ways of gleaning natural resources from the landscape and converting them into commodities and cash.

People often told me how lucky they felt to be from a place that allowed them such riches. Rather than depleting natural resources, given appropriate custodianship of the land, people felt they were entitled to usufructuary portions (see Chapter 4). Collecting antlers that had dropped off naturally didn't affect the balance of things and they resented externally imposed tariffs and restrictions. Local people were more aware than others of annual changes and paid close attention to any fluctuations in seasonal quantity or quality, being able to 'read' the environment in various ways (see below on milk and over-grazing, for example).[7]

Antler collection, however, defied normal economic conditions and emerged, almost as if by magic, out of nowhere. It involved an abundance in a time of scarcity as individuals searched of their own volition, in their own groups, motivated by chance rather than contract or certainty. As Tsing (2015) has noted for Matsutake mushroom-pickers, antler collection involves 'looking for your fortune, not doing your job' (Tsing 2015, 77). It was a kind of flight from salaried work (albeit such work is very rare in the countryside), and yet, ironically, local people speculated that the money for this activity was born out of central state authority – an outcome, a surplus perhaps, or accursed share, of a politician's need to clean money in time for the national election.

Gathering resources from the commons and turning them into commodities (what Tsing [2015] terms 'salvage accumulation') more often than not generate marginal, unpredictable and seasonal profits. More organised projects involve formal and informal loans and generate local forms of indebtedness as people work through known networks to facilitate their own and each other's lives.

Bread and milk businesses

The antler collection was uniquely intense. Delgermaa and her family were often preoccupied with other activities, facilitated through loans rather than funded by the finances of a single individual, but they also tended to be seasonally dependent, and so ran several projects throughout the year in order to be able to pay off different debts. Mostly, profit was born out of the conversion of existing things into commodities that could be bought and sold; the family were at the beginning of a supply chain of conversion.

In other writings I have focused on the success of Delgermaa's business endeavours (Empson 2011). A list at the end of this chapter details the different awards and medals she has received for her industry and entrepreneurship. I witnessed this when I spent the summers helping her receive milk from neighbouring families, weigh it, note the amount and pay for the milk. We then churned the milk through the milk machine, separating off the cream. The cream was saved in large containers underground, then sold for a profit in the city. The skimmed milk was used to make dried curds, which could be stored for longer periods and sold throughout the year (with inflated prices during New Year celebrations). I witnessed how Delgermaa managed to keep people involved in the chain, honouring debts and offering things in return. The milk-collecting business gradually expanded over 10 years and a bread-making business that involved less heavy work was added, enabling her husband to take part more. At one point she had two industrial electric ovens and employed several people. They would prepare the dough first thing in the morning, sell bread in the afternoon and have a new batch ready by the evening.

All this activity was successful in the sense that many people were involved, but it did not really accumulate much profit. I would look over Delgermaa's account books and note the quantity of 'in kind' exchanges that were waiting to be repaid. Unless they were crossed out, they hung there as a reminder of her swift generosity. In 2015 she lamented,

> I have been baking and selling bread for over three years in the district centre, but I have lost over MNT300,000 simply by *giving* [loaning] bread to people who have said they would pay me back later. I can't go running around asking for money for just one loaf of bread. I have to recognise that this is now lost and find the money some other way.

'Delayed barter', as Humphrey has pointed out, 'can only work in a relationship of knowledge and trust' (Humphrey 1985, 67). And yet, despite people knowing each other, in-kind payments continue as a form of exchange outside monetary transactions. Another way they tried to find the money to pay off these loans involved selling eggs and vegetables, and making cakes and special breads for New Year celebrations, as well as looking after four other people's cattle during the winter. The milk, the bread and the cattle-herding activities all demanded different inputs at different times of the year, but they sometimes complemented each other: in the winter she sold curds and bread and in the summer she concentrated on milk and cream.

Bank loans

Looking over my conversations with Delgermaa, I noted that in 2015 she still had three outstanding loans. Delgermaa explained,

> I have a 'household loan' [*örhiin zeeltei*] to make some things from flour products, like bread. It's for MNT4,500,000 and lasts for two years. The annual interest is 21.6 per cent. I pay MNT246,000 per month. We still have MNT1,980,000 outstanding on that. It is from Khaan Bank and, because we don't have much capital to put up as collateral, this is the only kind of loan that we can get [*tcr nögöö bur'tsaa horongö muu bolohoor*]. I also have a 'vegetable loan' [*nogoon' zeel*]. We got MNT1 million for the purchase of a greenhouse. This loan is for one year. I pay MNT153,000 per month for this one. We only have MNT300,000 left on that. I also have a

'pension loan'. It's for two or three years and the interest is 18 per cent, but this loan is from the State Bank. Everyone has a pension loan here [*bügd tetgevriin zeeltei*].

If loans are not paid back in the allotted time, banks threaten their customers with the requisition of their collateral, taking anything from milk and sewing machines to animals and houses. Delgermaa could only recall one such case, many years ago, although she had herself benefited from buying requisitioned property from the bank.[8] Loans were more easily accessible a few years ago, she lamented: 'The banks are granting fewer loans and it is rarer that people will get them. I guess it's to do with the economic crisis [*hyamraltai l holbootoi baih daa*].'

With banks granting fewer loans, people also had less collateral, lending more informally to each other (*huv' hünees avna*). These loans were considered tougher, Delgermaa explained, because their interest rates were very high, at 10 per cent per month (*sard arvan huviin hüütei*).[9]

> Now everyone has loans [*büh hün zeeltei*], everyone has debts and there is no money [*Bügd örtei. Möngö baihgü*]. Sometimes it feels OK, as everyone is in debt, but, of course, I do worry about my loans, as they are debts. Sometimes I can't sleep at night because I am anxious, thinking, what if I won't be able to pay them back.

It is both frustrating and disheartening to be invited to take out loans and at the same time to know that the market is so small that it is often impossible to sell enough to make a profit to even pay back the loan. This situation leads to complicated arrangements where one loan is taken to pay off another and so on, leading to entanglements of debt repayment that only a very skilled accountant can keep track of (see Waters 2016).[10] In-kind barter transactions bridge but also destabilise accounts. Another factor that plagued people at this time was the high cost of basic commodities, meaning that the elderly, for example, could not live off their pensions alone.[11] Delgermaa explained,

> People can't make savings because pensions are too low, leading people to take out loans against their pensions in order to pay for basic foodstuffs. There are many small entrepreneurs here, but due to the small market it's hard to sell things. The purchasing power is very bad, people always ask for things on loan and never repay you.

With only a small sector of society able to buy things, because of a lack of cash, the model of microfinance promoted by the banks just wasn't translating into anything like they imagined.

Insiders and outsiders of trade

When I talked with Delgermaa and her daughter, it became apparent that by 2015–16 the heyday of small business loans was over; with the larger economic downturn people were simply chasing ways to pay off debts.

> I pay one loan with the other one, and I don't have any profit. Due to my debts, I am not able to progress. When I produce things and want to sell them there aren't many people to buy, because there is no cash. People take bread and meat without paying directly, because they don't have money. So we just note it down. They don't return to pay me. I get flour from the shop as a loan, so my debt increases. When I get milk from someone, I pay for that, but when someone borrows cream from me and doesn't pay for that, my debts just increase.

Delgermaa's description of 'giving' and 'loaning' seemed complex and at times confusing. I asked her daughter to clarify what the Mongolian term was for giving someone something in exchange – what we might refer to as 'barter'. She replied, 'We call that "the exchange of goods [*baraa solilt-soo*], or barter [*baraa soliltsoh barter*]".'

From Delgermaa's and several of the local shop owners' account books it seemed that a huge proportion of transactions were exchanges that didn't directly involve money. Even if they did involve money there was often delayed payment. The exchange of commodities for foraged or locally produced goods was also common.[12] Delgermaa explained, 'We only do this kind of practice here, among each other [*tiimerhüü yum ene dotroo l baigaa*]. We don't do these kind of exchanges [*soliltsohgüi*] with strangers in Ulaanbaatar.'[13]

Clarifying the boundaries of who counts as insiders and outsiders for different kinds of exchange, Delgermaa set the limits of barter. This chimes with Humphrey's argument that barter is normally conducted between known people, who trust each other, and may emerge out of economic instability and the scarcity of money (Humphrey 1985, 65). Such limits constrained the trade they could do with outsiders, which was dependent on monetary transactions. However, barter did allow a greater circulation of things within the community, in which establishing the equivalence of things could be maintained and respected, even over long time periods. As in accounts of rural female entrepreneurs elsewhere, Delgermaa was always lending to some people and borrowing from others. The close-knit rural setting made lending more flexible and diverse than that experienced by Tuyaa, for example, who was located in the city (see Pelkmans and Umetbaeva 2018, 1060).

This situation was not simply born out of scarcity or a lack of money. Delgermaa explained that barter could also, at times, become the general economy: 'Some people are simply too lazy to make cream themselves, so they give me milk and I give them some cream in exchange. This works for us because from the milk we can make dried curds, so we both gain.'

As the economy slowed down and less money circulated, exchanges like this extended outwards. Traders in the city and provincial capital were now dependent on sales, rather than giving money upfront, to pay for things (a practice common at the beginning of the democratic period).

> Now when I put my products in the shops in Ulaanbaatar, I have to wait a long time until I get the money, sometimes several months later. Often the money is received little by little, like MNT30,000 today, MNT20,000 tomorrow, then MNT15,000 the day after, and so on. When I put some dairy products in the shops in Baganuur, for example, I only receive the money maybe a month later. Two years ago, we would bring the products and receive the money directly. Now there is a delay. Nobody has cash and everybody is in crisis [*büh hün möngögüi hyamrald orj baina sh dee*].

Although Delgermaa had succeeded in creating a thriving business selling bread, cream and curds, by 2016 it involved gathering raw materials from only three or four households, and most of the technical machinery they had purchased had been sold. This period coincided with Delgermaa's husband's physical decline and their increasing need to look after grandchildren; thus it was not just the threat of increasing debt and lack of money that meant they stopped. They managed to keep them going on a sufficient scale to be able to pay off their outstanding debts; but outstanding business loans meant that others in the district had to become herders to make repayments and get cash. Which brings us back to the point Delgermaa's husband made at the start of this chapter: herding has for many become a loan repayment scheme. In fact, much pasture degradation could directly result from the liberalisation of banks in countryside districts.

Chains of debt

One of the reasons Delgermaa was able to carry on for so long was that she had some steadfast friendships. They helped tide things over when life got tough and the margins were too small. Although interest rates among individual lenders were high – Delgermaa referred to almost being 'smashed' by repayments to one individual – one of her good friends, Altaa, often granted informal loans.

During the socialist period Altaa was one of two workers at the local agricultural bank distributing salaries and managing savings. In the 1990s she became a small-scale trader and sold goods – such as toilet paper, soap, white sugared nuts, waffles and clothes soap – from a small hut in her yard. In 2000 she opened the first big shop in the district. 'People used to come in when it first opened and say, "It even smells like a city shop!",' she commented proudly. At the same time as Altaa established her shop she also began to buy commodities like nuts and berries from local people. Her husband sold these for a profit in Ulaanbaatar and used the money to buy things to sell in the district shop.

After some years they were able to secure a permit to sell alcohol and cigarettes and this became a major source of their income. 'It went fine for about 10 years,' she comments, 'but now the pace of trade is bad [*odoo güilgee muu*].' Having purchased a flat in the city through a large bank loan, they plan to sell their shop in three or four years and move on.

Delgermaa benefited from borrowing flour from Altaa's shop, which she paid back once she had sold her bread. She was always reliable; if she couldn't make the money from her bread sales she'd find another way to raise the funds. Altaa managed many such debt arrangements in her shop. She had a drawer full of social security and pension books that she took as collateral against monetary loans, and her account books were full of notes detailing who owed what.[14]

When in the district, I always spent a few days sitting behind the counter with Altaa to observe these loan transactions and 'the ethical work carried out by the lenders and borrowers' (see Pelkmans and Umetbaeva 2018, 1050). In just one day her notebook recorded individual loans of MNT29,900, MNT88,710, MNT5000, MNT1810 and MNT800. Altaa explained, 'It's very hard just to ignore people when they come in and ask to have things. That woman is just standing there; I can't ignore her.'

She explained how people often seek loans in the early autumn to raise funds to send their children to school or university. In the spring she often grants pension loans. In the summer, when children return from school and university and many relatives are visiting, the sales in her shop are at their highest. In contrast the winter is slow and no one visits very often. I noticed how selective she was about whom she gave loans to. At first it seemed arbitrary, but I came to realise that it was always based on her assessment of their wider lives and economic situations. She knew whom she could count on to pay back later and whom she couldn't. When a young couple from the countryside came to get some essentials but couldn't pay her for a month, she let them take the things on chit. Such gestures appeared kind and generous and not at all exploitative.[15]

Temporary accumulation and dispersal

Rather than see the economic activities I have been describing as alternatives to, on the periphery of, or outside capitalism, we need to recognise that they are, in fact, the base, the norm, the ordinary and mainstream upon which much of the general economy in Mongolia flourishes. Of course, Mongolia is dependent on foreign direct investment, IMF loans and bailouts and the success of its mega-mines to generate royalties, but small business activities and exchanges, such as those explored in this chapter, drive the general pace of the economy for many. Attending to their creation – how items come into being as commodities, through what processes and via which relations they are exchanged – we can illuminate the particular form that capitalism is taking here and attend to the kinds of relations and subjects such forms generate. This point about co-constitution is important. Through it we see how people are shaped by wider economic processes, as well as shape them, as they act from particular situated perspectives, sometimes considered 'the periphery'.

In this and many district centres the gap between being a herder and a local entrepreneur is virtually non-existent; everyone juggles multiple ways of getting by. We must recognise the thoroughly modern activity that nomadic herding is, rather than relegating it to some kind of 'alternative' non-capitalist other (à la Gibson-Graham 2006, 1996). Their diverse activities criss-cross between the making of commodities and using resources from the commons to create variegated economic landscapes, such as those I have described, where money is used in certain exchanges and not in others. Tsing (2015, 66) argues that, instead of seeing these as alternatives to capitalism, we need to pay attention to the non-capitalist elements on which capitalism depends – that is, to the diversity that exists within capitalism itself.

This is an innovative suggestion because it requires us to attend to the way that capitalism is always dependent on turning natural resources, which were once commons available to everyone, into commodities that can be traded in a market. What Tsing terms 'salvage accumulation' is the process that makes the accumulation of things as commodities possible. The antlers required for money laundering, or the animal parts required for medicinal sales, or even the milk from cattle turned into curds and cream for sale in the city – through these things' accumulation and conversion they are given monetary value (Tsing 2015, 128). Salvage is thus a feature of how capitalism works, whether it be mineral resources extracted from the ground or pine nuts gathered in the forest. The sites from which they are gathered are simultaneously inside and outside, in what Tsing calls 'peri-capitalist locales' (Tsing 2015, 63). Making things into assets is a form of creativity and innovation, a bringing of things into being (see Tsing 2015, 271).

As we've seen, local people in this district perceive themselves as lucky (*az hishightei*) to be able to access resources from the landscape around them and turn these into desirable assets for others. They believe not that they have this opportunity through outright ownership (although herd animals are the property – *ömch* – of the herder), but that they are able to accumulate riches because they live in a place where they honour and respect their environment, gleaning resources (or appropriating their share) and converting them into items of value for wider commodity chains.[16] Not unlike the way items are granted on loan, in kind and on chit, within the district the logic of temporary possession, of access to a certain portion (through usufruct), scales from the intimacy of homes and shops into the vast landscape in which they are located (see Empson 2014).

One of the reasons these types of activities are so important for people living like this is that so much of their life is constantly changing. By 'change' I mean not just that seasonal activities and plans change, but also that things are perceived to be in flux economically and politically. Although people aspire to wider ideas of progress and development, particularly in the way their district is perceived by outsiders (such as having electricity, neatly marked roads, little or nearly no cow dung on the streets, clean schoolchildren, etc.), they live in anticipation that things may alter radically overnight and so they work together as wider family units and networks to support each other through such shifts.[17]

In this context we see, as Ledeneva (2006, 1) has described for post Soviet Russia, that the 'reorientation of the use of personal networks toward a new type of shortage – the shortage of money' – generates a new range of practices and exchanges (Ledeneva in Pelkmans and Umetbaeva 2018, 1053). The constant reinvention of the uses of existing alliances and networks means that life is lived in response to change. This kind of 'precarity … stimulates noticing, as one works with what is available' (Tsing 2015, 278). As we have seen, it also means knowing when to take risks – when to allow debt to accumulate, when to repay it and when to hedge one's bets and make changes – while at other times sticking things out and waiting.

Delgermaa and her family have survived by herding animals, by building houses and selling them to people in the city and by gathering nuts, antlers and other animal parts, supporting such activities with bank and personal loans that enable them to set up supply chains for bread, cream and curds and make a profit. It is important to recognise all this as a kind of work and a way of making a life. With a lack of cash in the general economy, however, more people are resorting to herding, particularly other people's animals, as a way to pay off the damage resulting from the liberalisation of the banking sector.[18] Through such arrangements people who are not registered in the district are able to rear their animals on the pastures, such as those now tended by Delgermaa's eldest sons, and the number of animals grazing in the district has increased. Overgrazing means less grass, and this, in turn, has an impact on the amount of milk produced by animals, thereby depleting resources overall. Herding has become, for many, nothing more than a loan repayment scheme.[19] Delgermaa lamented,

> Last year the milk was very strange. From August or even the end of July you can usually get one litre of cream out of 10 litres of milk; however, last summer it took 13, sometimes 15, litres of milk to get one litre of heavy cream. Cow milk has become very liquid [*ühriin süü tiim shingen bolchihson baina shüü dee*]. This is the condition we live in [*tiim bolzoltoi*].

Reflecting on these arrangements, Delgermaa and her husband sometimes regretted selling their herds. 'We don't have goats or animals of our own now, so we got caught in between these two things [*tiim tegeed dund n' ingeed hayagdchihaj baigaa baihgüi yu*].' This being caught in between is, again, reminiscent of the idea of the gap (as described in Chapter 1). It is exactly in such a space, I have argued, that we need to attend to what emerges. Delgermaa's resilience, her ability to survive precarity by being innovative and flexible, allowed new kinds of subjectivity to come into being, even if they have emerged within and among known networks and friends.

Reflections on the state of democracy

Being caught in between two things, living in response to flux and change, may be something one becomes used to and skilled at, but they also raise wider moral questions about the world one is being asked to live in. In my discussions with Delgermaa and her family and friends about the activities described above, our conversations often expanded to wider reflections about the state of the country. At the time, it had just been revealed that several MPs held personal offshore bank accounts containing millions of dollars, presumed to have been syphoned off from public resources.[20] From the ordinary people's perspective, politics and the economic situation they were experiencing were intimately intertwined, and this amounted to general disillusion with democracy as a way of organising society. Even Delgermaa's husband, a staunch democrat, now criticised the democrats: 'the democrats can't carry the state … it was actually better under socialism when we all had jobs … our country is becoming smaller and smaller as the Chinese are approaching'.

The general impression was that politicians did exactly what they wanted for their own gain (using the Mongolian phrase 'to pick the bone clean of any meat' [*möljih*]: taking all the wealth from the nation and people for themselves).[21] The concept of an offshore account was new to many Mongolians, and the revelations came as a shock as well as confirmation of the deep-seated lack of morality among the rich. 'And here, here, there is a big director at the top [the former minister of finance] with an offshore account, with one million dollars in it!' my friend Bold exclaimed. 'And he claims he simply forgot about it! Can you believe that? A Mongolian person forgot they had one million dollars! Just going about like that and forgetting. Do you understand? He had one million dollars and simply forgot about it!' With news like this, sparsely stocked shops, little cash circulating in the economy and elections soon approaching, people felt the need to think over what was happening and deliberate about what was to come next.

Events like the frantic antler collection become breaking points and openings – not quite 'decision-events' but moments when they speculated and gossiped about politics as they searched for meaning and connections in a world that they felt disconnected from. There was a sense that the work of trying to understand and make connections was necessary just to prove to oneself that one wasn't totally excluded. Nothing was known for certain, but speculation circulated about the reasons why certain decisions were made at the national level. Delgermaa's daughter, Baigal, reflected on this gap between official information and the world they found themselves in: 'State information is always false and doesn't reflect reality. The state statistical information from Ulaanbaatar, for example, is completely false. They claim that the average salary is MNT700,000 to MNT800,000, but everyone knows this is absolutely wrong; it's MNT430,000.'

In such a context most people distrusted the state in its current form. They distrusted the idea that more debt was a means to leverage oneself and the nation out of crisis. They lamented that the people 'at the top' (the politicians) had only followed the 'yellow heads' (*shar tolgoiton*), that is, the advice of Western investors and bankers, and 'could not find their seats'; they could not pull their act together. How were the people 'at the bottom' meant to follow such an example? There was only one way, Delgermaa's husband explained. What was necessary was to come together in your extended family and networks, to pool your resources and support each other.

*

This chapter has explored the edges of what we might think of as the economy to trace the way in which non-capitalist forms of value are constantly being converted into commodities that can be sold for money or traded for other things. The twists and turns of such activities are often beyond the control of the people doing the accumulating and so wider speculation arises as to why the market is the way it is and who are the people driving and shaping things. To attend to this speculation and critique is to listen to a politics that is just emerging and is formative of the affective atmosphere of everyday life (see Tsing 2015, 254). This opacity of knowledge, or 'fog' (*manan*, to use a metaphor commonly used in Mongolian political circles), leads Delgermaa and her friends to turn inwards to networks of local support, which connect and sustain like a web, holding people in place as the world moves – or jolts forwards at an unpredictable tempo.

Rather than relegate their experience to the periphery, I want to highlight that, for most, this is the ordinary. For the majority of people, not part of the tiny percentage of those who constitute the elite, their ways of strategising, speculating and 'reading' the economy are the norm. Their seeing and sensing what they can offer to existing commodity chains and knowing how to intervene in various kinds of markets is endlessly creative and inventive, but it also involves risks and chances that challenge ideas about 'stability' which some observers may take for granted. Rather than being stuck, or left out, in their constant adaptability they set the pace for wider forms of change enabling the emergence of new resilient subjectivities.

Notes

1. Delgermaa's medals and awards for the production of dairy and bakery products include: (1) Hödöö aj ahui Hünsnii Uildveriin tergüün (2012); (2) Niitiin aj ahui üilchilgeenii tergüün (2012); (3) Onon goliin sav gazriin shildeg üildverlegch emegtei (2012); (4) Mongol ulsiin üild-verchnii evleliin hündet temdeg (2012); (5) MAKH Namiin Hündet temdeg (nomerinh n' namin gishüün); (6) Ahmadyn aldar hündet temdeg (2013); (7) Batshireet Sumiin hödölmörch eej (2013); (8) Batshiretiin namar hündet temdeg (2016); (9) Ahmadiin aldar (2013).
2. He used two phrases to refer to the practice of paying back bank loans through herding: 'the meaning of life for herders is to pay back bank loans' (*bank tejeegch malchid*, literally 'herders feeding the banks') and 'Herders for the Banks' (*Banknii Malchid*). The result is many more animals on the pastureland.
3. Waters (2019, 216) talks about how the 'generalised rotation of debt' is also circulated out of social support in informal networks in the Mongolian countryside.
4. I thank Liz Fox for conversations about the way the Mongolian language allows just this differ-ence and repetition – a kind of formal structure that can be applied to any set of relations.
5. Later, when I returned to Ulaanbaatar, I had the chance to speak about this activity with some-one from the Ministry of Finance, who had a different interpretation. She wondered if it could have been driven by someone who had connections to people at customs, and they had wor-ried this situation could change once the elections had taken place, so they felt the need to conduct the business while their networks were still active and the people they knew still held powerful positions.
6. This involves putting something under the scale sheet to give it extra weight. 'When we look at the history of Chinese trade and money lending in Khalkh Mongolia, there are many examples of such fraudulent activities as short-counting and short-measuring' (Sanjdorj 1980, 92). For example, Sanjdorj explains that Chinese traders during this period had at least three different weights: a heavier one for buying, a lighter one for selling and a third correct one for when they were unable to cheat. Among these Chinese traders 'it was not considered cheating to take advantage of buyers ignorant of the true value and quality of goods' (Sanjdorj 1980, 92).
7. Resource-based extraction is also socially undergirded by concepts of fair prices on account of resource sacredness (see Waters 2019, 121, 172).
8. 'One year I bought a milk machine from them,' she said, 'but they never tell you the origin of where they've come from.'
9. 'Now everyone is in debt because they can't pick the pine nuts, the season is closed and they have no money,' Delgermaa explained, '[s]o there is no other way than to take out more loans.' Furthermore, illegal activities fuel loan repayments: 'People get rich, not depending on the livestock, you know. There must be a secret business. Yes, there might be a business of illegal tree logging, tree stealing. That's how there are houses built and sold secretly. People are fell-ing trees illegally without a permit [*goojin*] and selling the wood or wooden houses to the city to make money.'
10. Delgermaa's daughter told me, 'the thing you need to understand, Rebecca, is that the items sold and the money never adds up. There is always a loss, or some money missing, as people always take things on loan.'
11. In September 2015 1 kg of rice cost MNT2500, 1 kg of sugar cost MNT1800 and 25 kg of flour cost MNT29,000. Herders sold her their milk for MNT300 per litre, but in autumn the payment could increase to MNT1000. Cream cost MNT5000 per litre and butter MNT8000 per kg. Meat ranged from MNT4500 to MNT7500 for 1 kg. Pensions are usually around MNT200,000 a month (hers is MNT247,000 and her husband's was MNT227,000 per month).
12. This practice had existed during the socialist period, when skins of animals were sometimes exchanged for items available in the state shop (*sklad*). However, at that time exchanges were limited to those one knew well; to people within the local community. They were based on trust and an intimate knowledge of each other, where the shame of avoiding repayment mat-tered socially.
13. Delgermaa's daughter explained, 'You know, Rebecca, you can go to the shop and procure goods (such as bread, cigarettes and flour) by giving some fruits and berries that you have collected. You don't have to give money.'
14. Social security books are valuable because you cannot claim monthly child allowance with-out them.

15. Her son manages the shop, wiping money over the items to invite fortune and future sales, but even this does not distract from the fact that social connections underlie all the shop's transactions, which are not void of morally driven lending and debt (see Waters [2018, 411] on 'collateralising the social').

16. 'Even as entrepreneurs concentrate their private wealth through building alienation into commodities, they continue to draw from unrecognised entanglements. The thrill of private ownership is the fruit of an underground common' (Lowenhaupt Tsing 2015, 274).

17. Following Lowenhaupt Tsing (2015, 83), the idea of 'assemblage' might be better here than 'culture' to describe the open-ended and transformative entanglements of ways of being as new goal posts are created and aspired to in the light of wider changes.

18. A lot of pasture degradation in Mongolia is a direct result of the liberalisation of the banking sector in the 2000s, when bank loans became widely available. With the economic crisis from 2014, cash became less available and people were burdened with bank debts. This led to more people resorting to herding (very often other people's animals) to pay off bank loans.

19. This is a simplification of a situation that remains complex. First, the assumption that degradation results from increasing herd numbers is very difficult to disentangle from other drivers like climate change. Secondly, Daniel Murphy (2018) discusses how loans impact on herd size over time and we can see that loans are simply part of a whole host of factors that affect that linkage between financial liberalisation and pasture degradation.

20. This is an opinion further captured in the Buriad proverb recounted by Delgermaa's sister-in-law: 'A hard person carries the state [hatuu hün tör bar'dag] / A stingy person stores their wealth [haruu haramch hün zoor' bar'dag]'.

21. See: www.ft.com/content/9224cd16-3703-11e8-8eee-e06bde01c544.

22. For example, the Rostov developmental model, the socialist idea of progress and the Buddhist idea of Shambhala emerging out of the time of great calamities.

Interlude V

Batbold is 48 years old and lives in Ulaanbaatar. He is constantly moving between business projects as new visions of the future arise. He went on to study English and Russian at university in Odessa. Here he met a Mongolian woman, from a family of academics, who was studying economics. They married, and when they returned to Mongolia he needed to get out and make the world his own.

Property project 1: collapsed future

Batbold's career as an entrepreneur began by selling wool with a friend on the Mongolian–Chinese border. Later, his brother, who held a high position at the national copper mine, managed to get him a job with the Japanese company Samsung, which bought copper from the mine for their computers. After studying for an MBA, Batbold got a job selling their products in Mongolia. His office overlooked a small plot with a one-storey building and a few garages that seemed to be mostly unused. The plot next to it was also mostly empty.

Batbold and his friend combined their assets to buy this land in the early 2000s. Now, in 2014, they have erected five large buildings there, one of them with an impressive 16 storeys. The erection of these buildings involved imagining different kinds of visions of what their future use might be, and of the funds and means to create them. Batbold paid for architectural plans to be drawn up for the buildings and then sought funds to finance the developments. He secured various foreign investors and together they formed a company, which also included some relatives. The main building, envisaged as a hotel, was built by Chinese construction workers who worked under an Inner Mongolian foreman. Now the main building is finished, and a smaller four-storey building sits by its side.

When the economy sped up, the hotel was redesigned according to different imagined uses. With the economic downturn, however, the building was redesigned yet again, this time for office space. The foreign investors withdrew and refused to grant more money, so a new buyer was found in the form of a Mongolian bank. Through the sale Batbold can finish the construction of the building and pay the funders their different shares. It is envisaged that the bank will then sell or rent part of the building to a management consultancy company that will have its offices there.

Property project 2: future hoped for

A related project involves his textile factory, which has a different temporal trajectory. During the socialist period this factory was owned by the state. With the collapse of socialism, shares in the factory were assigned to its workers, but it remained unused for many years. Over several years Batbold acquired shares through personal connections, but also by purchasing them on the stock market. He now owns 80 per cent of the factory but still needs to buy out the remaining shareholders with money gained from the sale of the building mentioned above; this may take several years. In the meantime, and with his experience of selling and buying wool, the factory is being run by a relative of his and producing textiles, which they sell to Russian and European companies which then put their own logos on them.

The factory building has become smaller and they use less of the space, but lots of the old machines are still working. The land owned as part of the factory site is large, and it is becoming increasingly obvious that this location, once considered to be on the outskirts of the city, will soon become a highly desirable residential area inside the city. Batbold hopes not only to continue with the textile business, but in the future to develop this land in various ways, such as selling it to developers to build houses or shopping malls.

Property project 3: futures realised

Another vision for the future is materialised in the properties that Batbold and his family have lived in for the last 20 or so years. As a young family, they inherited a flat from his wife's parents, who had been allocated an apartment according to their work during the socialist period. Selling this to Batbold's sister, they bought a newly built two-storey house in the centre of town within a partially gated area. This modern complex was highly desirable and populated by elites, but when pollution began to increase Batbold and his friends sought a new place for their families to live. They invested again in (unbuilt) properties in an exclusive area to the south, by the mountains, selling their old house to a relative. After they had lived there for several years the traffic became increasingly tricky and the area overpopulated, so they invested in a new architectural vision by the main river that runs through the city. They now live here and enjoy the peace and quiet and the clean air, but no public transport and little other infrastructure has been developed in this area.

Folded temporalities and the coexistence of economic times

As I mentioned in the Introduction, one might say that prophecy, or any kind of vision of the future, tells us more about what is desired in the present than it does about how that future will unfold. Although some may say that it does structure action, recent critiques of performative economic models have shown that these are never seamless; there is always a slippage or gap between the future imagined and the experience that actually comes into being. In fact, multiple models of the future may be held in mind simultaneously.[22] How people move between these and act on them in the present is not always easy to trace, especially if these futures are not seen as desired endpoints by one's interlocutors.

Though economic reforms within the model of a free market may be an ideal template for many Euro-American ideas of progress, it is one that many Mongolians are increasingly coming to perceive as problematic. As highlighted by Miyazaki's informant Tada (Miyazaki 2006), a sense of hope in the global financial markets has been dampened, and doubt about predictions has given rise to critique. While Batbold is trying to sell his half-finished hotel to pay off his foreign investors and complete the building work, the bank he hopes to sell it to is also planning to sell it on to someone else. Multiple dreams within dreams! Extracting oneself from these webs of debt and the futures they imply is a tricky business with many potential pitfalls.

Maurer (2012) points out that anthropologists have an important lesson to learn from local critiques of contemporary capitalism:

> … there is much more to 'economy' than the tip of the iceberg that we see at the mode: wage labour and surplus accumulation. There is also slavery, gifting, barter, non-monetised labour, and so on … The point is not naively to celebrate this plurality or diversity in economy or finance. It is instead to ask how participants make alternatives and how those alternatives, once specified and rendered

objects of reflexive knowledge, oscillate in and out of phase with the central tendency, and what aspects of them continue to pro-duce dissonant vibrations even in phase with that mode. People do not 'do' one mode of finance or another mode of finance; they pro-ductively engage in and perform a plurality, thus blurring the line between alternative and dominant, formal and informal, embed-ded and disembedded, or any of the familiar dichotomies that have animated so much critical scholarship on economy and finance. (Maurer 2012, 415)

Such modes – which reverberate simultaneously – may be conceived as paral-lel economic temporalities that come to orient action. In architectural contexts we see how future visions are manifested in physical form. The future becomes something brought into the present, made visible physically in present time. Here we can begin to think about the idea that the future is always a way of speaking about the present, a wish-fulfilment articulated in the now, a kind of fractal ontology or skyline (O'Sullivan 2010). Batbold jumps between these modes in his parallel projects. In doing so they manifest a varigated skyline of temporal, economic, or physical forms that provide the infrastructure for future manifestations and articulations (Maurer 2013).

Conclusion

As an anthropologist, I came to economic anthropology somewhat illegitimately, through research on prophecy (Empson 2006), kinship and ownership regimes (Empson 2011; 2012). Performative economic theory gave me a way in to explore forms of financialisation that were impacting on the lives of people in my long-term field site (Empson 2014). This led to broader interests in issues of temporary possession (Empson and Bonilla 2019). During the course of my research for this book my theoretical interest was again pushed to look beyond ideas of performativity to feminist scholars who were calling into question the very idea of what counts as the economic, by extending these concepts to examine broader issues of care, hope, debt and freedom. They called attention to the way in which the economy is made at the margins of what we may think of as its reach.

This broadening of focus has been liberating in that it has opened up what counts as a 'proper subject' in the study of economic anthropology. It has shifted the focus from pure representation (a sort of thick description) and relativism (a deep substantivist approach: 'the economy can be anything') to look at the way diversity actually underpins the foundations of what we think of as capitalism.

This commitment to highlighting diversity within is, in itself, a practice of prefiguration, both for anthropologists and for their subjects, bringing the political into anthropological writing, so that choosing what to highlight and describe works to amplify and make that world come into being. Terms like 'capitalism' and 'the economy' carry theoretical baggage, which I have tried to break apart through ethnographic insight that brings new subjects to bear on these themes. Foremost of these is the concept of the gap, a term that was used ethnographically but which I have found useful when mobilised across the chapters to think conceptually about the different issues that arise for each of the women. Not unlike the idea of 'the void', the gap is as much a space as a temporal concept that allows an exchange of perspectives, a looking back and revising past ideas in light of the present; a revision based on how things have turned out. Rather than (re)creating accounts of homogeneous neoliberal conditions, I have chosen to focus on the way in which this perspective opens us up to a diversity of lives.

We have seen how this diversity is realised through each of the chapters: as Oyunaa revised her past ideas about how to carry out a business in the present; as Sara reviewed her political ideas through an awareness of the need for radical change; through the way Tuyaa prefigures the future in her ethical calculus; in the way Zedlen, caught in socialist morals, is nevertheless able to exercise a freedom in her present work; and, finally, with Delgermaa, who resorts to networks of support when models from elsewhere fail to materialise the worlds they imagine. The world in which they act, which gives them, or limits, their agency, allows them to prefigure a trajectory over which they have some command. In these spaces the binaries on which the gap depends dissolve in the very act of reflecting back. Recognising that 'this space' has come to resemble something completely different, we generate a new third perspective or space. This final section is my own attempt at exactly that process.

The kind of world we have been looking at is one where people have questioned the legitimacy of the people who are leading their country. It is one where people resort to exchange in groups, and among networks or factions, when economic scarcity has brought a halt to the flow of things. Where democracy is seen as a system that facilitates corruption and greed, but people still strive for change, although they recognise that the path is not linear. Where trade with foreign investors, increasing reliance on sovereign debt, and the influence of the internet and the media have had an impact on the range of cosmological thought, allowing people to draw on practices and ideas from elsewhere to rethink things, including ideas about the nation. Alongside this looking outwards there is also a drawing inwards, not least because the geological and environmental landscape of Mongolia as it is exposed to new forms of extraction increasingly 'acts back' on those who live there, to expose polluted rivers, overgrazed pastureland, insurmountable waste and collapsing underground tunnels. A kind of geological and environmental retaliation intervenes in the progressive expansion of capitalism everywhere, but it is perhaps felt acutely in a country like Mongolia, where people live embedded in their environment in ways we may not quite do in the West (see Lee et al. 2019).

It is possible that what counts as a 'strategic resource' will shift away from the familiar mines and mineral reserves enshrined in laws as people around the world look to other ways to produce energy; that the pursuit of economic growth through extraction will not be the only model worth chasing. What will Mongolia's resources be then, and who will have access to them, and on what terms? A major cultural resource that has allowed people to manage the temporary and shifting, so prevalent over the past few years, is recourse to the master/custodian relationship (Empson 2014), which is not one of coloniser/colonised, but a form of access to resources based on nested hierarchies of usufruct, allowing people to navigate complex ownership relations, including ones based on debt and loans (see Chapters 4 and 5). By attending to the way in which such ideas are revised and reset, to the gap as a productive space of creativity and openness, we have been able to see how ideas about access and ownership may be mobilised as resources to rethink things for the future.

What does recognition of this say about the nature of global capitalism more generally? Throughout the wider project on which this book was based, I was often called upon to reflect on my findings to the Mongolian government, its banks and its business investors, as well as other governments. Sometimes I highlighted that what people were experiencing in Mongolia provided a kind of blueprint for what was beginning to happen elsewhere as economic policies in one place reverberated across borders, between East and West. At other times I emphasised that life for people in Mongolia has been shaped in very particular ways. This difference tells us something about how different forms of financialisation are received and shaped, and how developing economies are forced to accept certain structural policies but cannot always act on them in the same way as more developed countries, because the structures of power and finance that might buttress them do not exist. It is important to note the kinds of critique that emerge in such spaces and to document the 'non-scalable economic diversity' they engender. Not just to demonstrate ethnographic diversity but also to uncover the structural reasons why policies based on developmental economics do not translate in the way that may have been intended. It is to politically 'talk back' to those policies with the voices and experiences of the subjects who have had to live them.

In some ways the strategies my subjects have mobilised in 'the gap' will be familiar to anthropologists of Mongolia. They include, but are not confined to, reliance on networks, the economy of favours, drawing on the 'deep past' for religious, spiritual and nationalist ideas in times of uncertainty, expressions of ethical care and self-cultivation, and the sharing of ownership, assets and debt. I hope that these strategies, and others I've discussed, can also 'talk back' and be mobilised as critiques by anthropologists in their descriptions (and in answer to questions about their findings), so that a transfer of ideas occurs across perspectives. Documenting all this in writing is therefore a political act that broadcasts how people engage with economic volatility as a major characteristic of life, and not necessarily as a deviant or passing phase. The strategies mobilised by one's interlocutors can become a form of critique outside the sphere in which it is generated, speaking to different outcomes and audiences and working back on our own ideas of what are considered acceptable means of accumulating, owning and transacting (cf. Miyazaki 2006).

Finally – and I may not have been able to show the extent of this in this book – I want to stress that what we see materialising in the gap, in the space between an economic and a political vision and its slow unfurling into something else, is particular to Mongolia, but it also starkly holds up a mirror up to what is also materialising elsewhere. It may seem to some that I have been documenting the experiences of people exploited on the peripheries of world power, but their experiences demonstrate inequalities that are occurring in many places. With the flow of resources like coal and copper to China we can see the traces of larger migratory flows of global commodities, mineral wealth, political forms and social imaginaries. The goods we have come to rely on in the West carry more than their simple parts. They bind and implicate us in a chain of relations that stem back to the worlds I have been describing. In a parallel to the way in which Mongolian minerals continue to fuel China's steel industry, which satisfies the consumption of goods in the West, Mongolia's current economic experience and the subjects that emerge therewith should provide a basis for reflecting on our own need for change. Far from being something only undergone by those on the periphery, what is happening in Mongolia may, in fact, prefigure a future that we have yet to fully realise. Here we can begin to perceive final a reciprocity of perspectives. The West as a figure or exemplar of how politics and the economy 'should' run has finally become the ground as emerging Eastern economic subjects and their critiques begin to prefigure what we may come to experience in the West. That I learnt this from the five women who feature in this book makes me feel both extremely grateful and humbled.

It is with this insight that I want to end by saying that the gap that continues to hold our lives partially connected across different places reciprocates in multiple ways, allowing each of us to see a different world from that in which we are located and to prefigure our own futures in its image.

Bibliography

Appel, Hannah. 2017. 'Toward an Ethnography of the National Economy', *Cultural Anthropology* 32 (2): 294–322.

Austin, J.L. 1975. *How to Do Things with Words*. 2nd ed. Oxford: Clarendon Press.

Batsuuri, H. 2015. 'Original Sin: Is Mongolia Facing an External Debt Crisis?', *Northeast Asian Economic Review* 3 (2): 3–15.

Bear, Laura. 2015. *Navigating Austerity: Currents of Debt along a South Asian River*. Stanford, CA: Stanford University Press.

Bear, Laura. 2016. 'The LSE Platform: Communicating Inequalities', panel at Hay Festival, 29 May. https://www.hayfestival.com/p-10744-mike-savage-john-hills-laura-bear.aspx.

Bear, Laura, Karen Ho, Anna Lowenhaupt Tsing and Sylvia Yanagisako. 2015. 'Gens: A Feminist Manifesto for the Study of Capitalism', *Fieldsights*, 30 March. https://culanth.org/fieldsights/gens-a-feminist-manifesto-for-the-study-of-capitalism.

Berlant, Lauren. 2011. *Cruel Optimism*. Durham, NC: Duke University Press.

Berlin, Isaiah. 2013. 'Montesquieu'. In *Against the Current: Essays in the History of Ideas*, edited by Henry Hardy, 164–203. 2nd ed. Princeton, NJ: Princeton University Press.

Biehl, João. 2005. *Vita: Life in a Zone of Social Abandonment*. Berkeley: University of California Press.

Bonilla, Lauren. 2014. 'Extractive Infrastructures: Social, Territorial, and Institutional Transformations in Mongolia's Emerging Mining Economy'. PhD thesis, Clark University.

Borup, Mads, Nik Brown, Kornelia Konrad and Harro Van Lente. 2006. 'The Sociology of Expectations in Science and Technology', *Technology Analysis and Strategic Management* 18 (3–4): 285–98.

Butler, Judith. 1988. 'Performative Acts and Gender Constitution: An Essay in Phenomenology and Feminist Theory', *Theatre Journal* 40 (4): 519–31.

Buyandelger, Manduhai. 2013. *Tragic Spirits: Shamanism, Memory, and Gender in Contemporary Mongolia*. Chicago: University of Chicago Press.

Byambajav, Dalaibuyan. 2015. 'The River Movements' Struggle in Mongolia', *Social Movement Studies* 14 (1): 92–7.

Callon, Michel. 2008. 'What Does It Mean to Say that Economics Is Performative?' In *Do Economists Make Markets? On the Performativity of Economics*, edited by Donald MacKenzie, Fabian Muniesa and Lucia Siu, 311–57. Princeton, NJ: Princeton University Press.

Channell-Justice, Emily. 2019. 'Beyond the Soviet Slot', *Anthropology News*, 28 August. DOI: 10.1111/AN.1250.

Chuluunbat, Narantuya and Rebecca Empson. 2018. 'Networks and the Negotiation of Risk: Making Business Deals and People among Mongolian Small and Medium Businesses', *Central Asian Survey* 37 (3): 419–37.

Comaroff, Jean and John L. Comaroff. 1999. 'Occult Economies and the Violence of Abstraction: Notes from the South African Postcolony', *American Ethnologist* 26 (2): 279–303.

Deleuze, Gilles. 2006. *The Fold: Leibniz and the Baroque*, translated by Tom Conley. London: Continuum.

Doojav, Gan-Ochir. 2019. 'Mongolia's Growth Challenges', *East Asia Forum*, 6 July. www.eastasiaforum.org/2019/07/06/mongolias-growth-challenges/.

Dulam, Bumochir. 2018a. 'Generating Capitalism for Independence in Mongolia', *Central Asian Survey* 37 (3): 357–71.

Dulam, Bumochir. 2018b. 'Mongolia'. In *Routledge Handbook of Civil Society in Asia*, edited by Akihiro Ogawa, 95–109. London: Routledge.

Dulam, Bumochir. 2020. *The State, Popular Mobilisation and Gold Mining in Mongolia: Shaping 'Neo-Liberal' Policies*. London: UCL Press.

Economist, The. 2012. 'Booming Mongolia: Mine, All Mine', 21 January. www.economist.com/briefing/2012/01/21/mine-all-mine?zid=306&ah=1b164dbd43b0cb27ba0d4c3b12a5e227.

Empson, Rebecca, ed. 2006. *Time, Causality and Prophecy in the Mongolian Cultural Region: Visions of the Future*. Folkestone: Global Oriental.

Empson, Rebecca M. 2011. *Harnessing Fortune: Personhood, Memory, and Place in Mongolia*. Oxford: Oxford University Press.

Empson, Rebecca. 2012. 'The Dangers of Excess: Accumulating and Dispersing Fortune in Mongolia', *Social Analysis* 56 (1): 117–32.

Empson, Rebecca. 2014. 'An Economy of Temporary Possession'. Malinowski Memorial Lecture, London School of Economics, 22 May.

Empson, R. A. (2014). 'Portioning loans: cosmologies of wealth and power in Mongolia'. In *Framing Cosmologies The Anthropology of Worlds*. Manchester University Press, edited by Allen Abramson and Martin Holbraad.

Empson, Rebecca and Lauren Bonilla. 2019. 'Temporary Possession', *Fieldsights*, 29 March. https://culanth.org/fieldsights/series/temporary-possession.

Englund, Harri and James Leach. 2000. 'Ethnography and the Meta-narratives of Modernity', *Current Anthropology* 41 (2): 225–48.

Evans, Brad and Julian Reid. 2014. *Resilient Life: The Art of Living Dangerously*. Cambridge: Polity Press.

Fortun, Kim. 2014. 'From Latour to Late Industrialism', *HAU: Journal of Ethnographic Theory* 4 (1): 309–29.

Foucault, Michel. 1982. 'The Subject and Power', *Critical Inquiry* 8 (4): 777–95.

Fox, Elizabeth. 2019. 'Between Iron and Coal: Enacting Kinship, Bureaucracy and Infrastructure in the Ger Districts of Ulaanbaatar'. PhD thesis, University College London.

Garcia, Angela. 2010. *The Pastoral Clinic: Addiction and Dispossession along the Rio Grande*. Berkeley: University of California Press.

Gibson-Graham, J.K. 1996. *The End of Capitalism (As We Knew It): A Feminist Critique of Political Economy*. Oxford: Blackwell.

Gibson-Graham, J.K. 2006. *A Postcapitalist Politics*. Minneapolis: University of Minnesota Press.

Gibson-Graham, J.K. 2014. 'Rethinking the Economy with Thick Description and Weak Theory', *Current Anthropology* 55 (Supplement 9): S147–53.

Gilbert, Paul. 2015. 'Book Review – *Making Other Worlds Possible: Performing Diverse Economies*, edited by Gerda Roelvink, Kevin St Martin and J.K. Gibson-Graham', *LSE Review of Books*, 12 November. https://blogs.lse.ac.uk/lsereviewofbooks/2015/11/12/book-review-making-other-worlds-possible-performing-diverse-economies-edited-by-gerda-roelvink-kevin-st-martin-and-j-k-gibson-graham/.

Gilio-Whitaker, Dina. 2019. '173 – Dina Gilio-Whitaker', *Cultures of Energy*, 18 April. https://luminarypodcasts.com/listen/cenhs-at-rice-256/cultures-of-energy/173-dina-gilio-whitaker/39b79d02-e17a-4c44-80ca-84b8fa07f264.

Giménez Aliaga, Victor. 2017. 'Whose Populism? Which Democracy?', *Anthropology News* 58 (3): e79–85.

Graeber, David. 2012. 'The Sword, the Sponge, and the Paradox of Performativity: Some Observations on Fate, Luck, Financial Chicanery, and the Limits of Human Knowledge', *Social Analysis* 56 (1): 25–42.

Graeber, David. 2014. 'Anthropology and the Rise of the Professional-Managerial Class', *HAU: Journal of Ethnographic Theory* 4 (3): 73–88.

Guyer, Jane I. 2007. 'Prophecy and the Near Future: Thoughts on Macroeconomic, Evangelical, and Punctuated Time', *American Ethnologist* 34 (3): 409–21.

Han, Clara. 2011. 'Symptoms of Another Life: Time, Possibility, and Domestic Relations in Chile's Credit Economy', *Cultural Anthropology* 26 (1): 7–32.

Han, Clara. 2012. *Life in Debt: Times of Care and Violence in Neoliberal Chile*. Berkeley: University of California Press.

Henig, David and Nicolette Makovicky, eds. 2017. *Economies of Favour after Socialism*. Oxford: Oxford University Press.

Hickel, Jason. 2015. 'The Microfinance Delusion: Who Really Wins?', *Guardian*, 10 June. www.theguardian.com/global-development-professionals-network/2015/jun/10/the-microfinance-delusion-who-really-wins.

High, Mette M. 2017. *Fear and Fortune: Spirit Worlds and Emerging Economies in the Mongolian Gold Rush*. Ithaca, NY: Cornell University Press.

Ho, Karen. 2018. 'Markets, Myths, and Misrecognitions: Economic Populism in the Age of Financialization and Hyperinequality', *Economic Anthropology* 5 (1): 148–50.

Højer, Lars. 2004. 'The Anti-social Contract: Enmity and Suspicion in Northern Mongolia', *Cambridge Journal of Anthropology* 24 (3): 41–63.

Højer, Lars. 2012. 'The Spirit of Business: Pawnshops in Ulaanbaatar', *Social Anthropology* 20 (1): 34–49.

Holmes, Douglas, R. 2009. 'Economy of Words', *Cultural Anthropology* 24 (3): 381–419.

Hook, Leslie. 2012. 'Mongolia Flooded with Millionaires', *Financial Times*, 19 June. www.ft.com/content/d20bfd5e-b866-11e1-a2d6-00144feabdc0.

Hsu, Hua. 2019. 'Affect Theory and the New Age of Anxiety: How Lauren Berlant's Cultural Criticism Predicted the Trumping of Politics', *New Yorker*, 25 March. www.newyorker.com/magazine/2019/03/25/affect-theory-and-the-new-age-of-anxiety.

Humphrey, Caroline. 1983. 'Book Review – *Manchu Chinese Colonial Rule in Northern Mongolia*, by M. Sanjdorj, translated from Mongolian by Urgunge Onon', *Modern Asian Studies* 17 (1): 165–7.

Humphrey, Caroline. 1985. 'Barter and Economic Disintegration', *Man* 20 (1): 48–72.

Humphrey, Caroline. 1992. 'The Moral Authority of the Past in Post-socialist Mongolia', *Religion, State and Society* 20 (3–4): 375–89.

Humphrey, Caroline. 1993. 'Women, Taboo and the Suppression of Attention'. In *Defining Females: The Nature of Women in Society*, edited by Shirley Ardener, 73–92. Oxford: Berg.

Humphrey, Caroline. 1997. 'Exemplars and Rules: Aspects of the Discourse of Moralities in Mongolia'. In *The Ethnography of Moralities*, edited by Signe Howell, 25–47. London: Routledge.

Humphrey, Caroline. 2008. 'Reassembling Individual Subjects: Events and Decisions in Troubled Times', *Anthropological Theory* 8 (4): 357–80.

Humphrey, Caroline. 2012. 'Favors and "Normal Heroes": The Case of Postsocialist Higher Education', *HAU: Journal of Ethnographic Theory* 2 (2): 22–41.

Humphrey, Caroline and Urgunge Onon. 1996. *Shamans and Elders: Experience, Knowledge, and Power among the Daur Mongols*. Oxford: Clarendon Press.

Humphrey, Caroline and David Sneath, eds. 1996. *Culture and Environment in Inner Asia, Volume 1: The Pastoral Economy and the Environment*. Cambridge: White Horse Press.

Humphrey, Caroline and David Sneath. 1999. *The End of Nomadism? Society, State and the Environment in Inner Asia*. Durham, NC: Duke University Press.

Jackson, Michael. 2013. *The Politics of Storytelling: Variations on a Theme by Hannah Arendt*. 2nd ed. Copenhagen: Museum Tusculanum Press.

Jacobs, Michael and Mariana Mazzucato. 2016. 'Rethinking Capitalism: An Introduction'. In *Rethinking Capitalism: Economics and Policy for Sustainable and Inclusive Growth*, edited by Michael Jacobs and Mariana Mazzucato, 1–27. Chichester: Wiley-Blackwell.

Kaplonski, Christopher. 2004. *Truth, History and Politics in Mongolia: The Memory of Heroes*. London: RoutledgeCurzon.

Katsambekis, Giorgos. 2017. 'The Populist Surge in Post-democratic Times: Theoretical and Political Challenges', *Political Quarterly* 88 (2): 202–10.

Ker, Peter. 2019. 'How Rio Tinto Dug Itself a Hole in Mongolia', *Financial Review*, 8 July. www.afr.com/companies/mining/how-rio-tinto-dug-itself-a-hole-in-mongolia-20190702-p523gk.

Kohn, Michael. 2017. 'Mongolia Clears Hurdles Needed for $5.5 Billion IMF-Led Bailout', *Bloomberg News*, 20 April. www.bloomberg.com/news/articles/2017-04-19/mongolia-clears-hurdles-needed-for-5-5-billion-imf-led-bailout.

Laclau, Ernesto. 2005. *On Populist Reason*. London: Verso.

Laidlaw, James. 2002. 'For an Anthropology of Ethics and Freedom', *Journal of the Royal Anthropological Institute* 8 (2): 311–32.

Leach, James. 2002. 'Drum and Voice: Aesthetics and Social Process on the Rai Coast of Papua New Guinea', *Journal of the Royal Anthropological Institute* 8 (4): 713–34.

Ledeneva, Alena V. 1998. *Russia's Economy of Favours: Blat, Networking and Informal Exchange*. Cambridge: Cambridge University Press.

Ledeneva, Alena V. 2006. *How Russia Really Works: The Informal Practices that Shaped Post-Soviet Politics and Business*. Ithaca, NY: Cornell University Press.

Lee, Eun Jung, Dongfan Piao, Cholho Song, Jiwon Kim, Chul-Hee Lim, Eunji Kim, Jooyeon Moon, Menas Kafatos, Munkhnsan Lamchin, Seong Woo Jeon and Woo-Kyun Lee. 2019. 'Assessing Environmentally Sensitive Land to Desertification Using MEDALUS Method in Mongolia', *Forest Science and Technology* 15 (4): 210–20.

Lhamsuren, Munkh-Erdene. 2006. 'The Mongolian Nationality Lexicon: From the Chinggisid Lineage to Mongolian Nationality (from the Seventeenth to the Early Twentieth Century)', *Inner Asia* 8 (1): 51–98.

Lindquist, Johan. 2015. 'Of Figures and Types: Brokering Knowledge and Migration in Indonesia and Beyond', *Journal of the Royal Anthropological Institute* 21 (S1): 162–77.

Lkhaajav, Bolor. 2017. 'Mongolia's Democracy under Stress', *Diplomat*, 14 April. https://thediplomat.com/2017/04/mongolias-democracy-under-stress/.

Lowenhaupt Tsing, Anna. 2015. *The Mushroom at the End of the World: On the Possibility of Life in Capitalist Ruins*. Princeton, NJ: Princeton University Press.

MacKenzie, Donald, Fabian Muniesa and Lucia Siu. 2008. 'Introduction'. In *Do Economists Make Markets? On the Performativity of Economics*, edited by Donald MacKenzie, Fabian Muniesa and Lucia Siu, 1–19. Princeton, NJ: Princeton University Press.

Maurer, Bill. 2012. 'The Disunity of Finance: Alternative Practices to Western Finance'. In *The Oxford Handbook of the Sociology of Finance*, edited by Karin Knorr Cetina and Alex Preda, 413–30. Oxford: Oxford University Press.

Maurer, Bill. 2013. 'Transacting Ontologies: Kockelman's Sieves and a Bayesian Anthropology', *HAU: Journal of Ethnographic Theory* 3 (3): 63–75.

Mitchell, Timothy. 2005. 'The Work of Economics: How a Discipline Makes Its World', *European Journal of Sociology* 46 (2): 297–320.

Miyazaki, Hirokazu. 2006. 'Economy of Dreams: Hope in Global Capitalism and Its Critiques', *Cultural Anthropology* 21 (2): 147–72.

Murphy, Daniel J. 2018. '"We're Living from Loan-to-Loan": Pastoral Vulnerability and the Cashmere-Debt Cycle in Mongolia'. In *Individual and Social Adaptations to Human Vulnerability*, edited by Donald C. Wood, 7–30. Bingley: Emerald.

Myadar, Orhon and Sara Jackson. 2018. 'Contradictions of Populism and Resource Extraction: Examining the Intersection of Resource Nationalism and Accumulation by Dispossession in Mongolia', *Annals of the American Association of Geographers* 109 (2): 361–70.

Navaro, Yael. 2017. 'Diversifying Affect', *Cultural Anthropology* 32 (2): 209–14.

Navaro-Yashin, Yael. 2009. 'Affective Spaces, Melancholic Objects: Ruination and the Production of Anthropological Knowledge', *Journal of the Royal Anthropological Institute* 15 (1): 1–18.

Nielsen, Morten. 2014. 'The Negativity of Times: Collapsed Futures in Maputo, Mozambique', *Social Anthropology* 22 (2): 213–26.

Ortner, Sherry B. 2016. 'Dark Anthropology and Its Others: Theory since the Eighties', *HAU: Journal of Ethnographic Theory* 6 (1): 47–73.

O'Sullivan, Simon. 2010. 'Fold'. In *The Deleuze Dictionary*, edited by Adrian Parr, 107–8. Rev. ed. Edinburgh: Edinburgh University Press.

O'Sullivan, Simon. 2012. *On the Production of Subjectivity: Five Diagrams of the Finite–Infinite Relation*. Basingstoke: Palgrave Macmillan.

Pedersen, Morten Axel. 2011. *Not Quite Shamans: Spirit Worlds and Political Lives in Northern Mongolia*. Ithaca, NY: Cornell University Press.

Pedersen, Morten Axel. 2012. 'A Day in the Cadillac: The Work of Hope in Urban Mongolia', *Social Analysis* 56 (2): 136–51.

Pelkmans, Mathijs and Damira Umetbaeva. 2018. 'Moneylending and Moral Reasoning on the Capitalist Frontier in Kyrgyzstan', *Anthropological Quarterly* 91 (3): 1049–74.

Petrović-Šteger, Maja. 2019. 'Stepping out of Duration: Timescripting and Practices of Resourcing in Serbia'. Paper presented at *What Futures Belong to Our Present? Anthropology on the Configurations of Imagination*, Ljubljana, 12 September.

Plueckhahn, Rebekah. 2020. *Shaping Urban Futures in Mongolia: Ulaanbaatar, Dynamic Ownership and Economic Flux*. London: UCL Press.

Plueckhahn, Rebekah and Bumochir Dulam. 2018. 'Capitalism in Mongolia: Ideology, Practice and Ambiguity', *Central Asian Survey* 37 (3): 341–56.

Povinelli, Elizabeth A. 2011. 'Introduction: The Child in the Broom Closet'. In *Economies of Abandonment: Social Belonging and Endurance in Late Liberalism*, by Elizabeth A. Povinelli, 1–46. Durham, NC: Duke University Press.

Radchenko, Sergey and Mendee Jargalsaikhan. 2017. 'Mongolia in the 2016–17 Electoral Cycle: The Blessings of Patronage', *Asian Survey* 57 (6): 1032–57.

Rajković, Ivan. 2018. 'For an Anthropology of the Demoralized: State Pay, Mock-Labour, and Unfreedom in a Serbian Firm', *Journal of the Royal Anthropological Institute* 24 (1): 47–70.

Rawski, Evelyn S. 1998. *The Last Emperors: A Social History of Qing Imperial Institutions*. Berkeley: University of California Press.

Reid, Julian. 2012. 'The Neoliberal Subject: Resilience and the Art of Living Dangerously', *Revista Pléyade* 10: 143–65.

Riessman, Catherine Kohler. 2005. 'Narrative Analysis'. In *Narrative, Memory, and Everyday Life*, edited by Nancy Kelly, Christine Horrocks, Kate Milnes, Brian Roberts and David Robinson, 1–7. Huddersfield: University of Huddersfield.

Robbins, Joel. 2012. 'On Becoming Ethical Subjects: Freedom, Constraint, and the Anthropology of Morality', *Anthropology of this Century* 5. http://aotcpress.com/articles/ethical-subjects-freedom-constraint-anthropology-morality/.

Robbins, Joel. 2013. 'Beyond the Suffering Subject: Toward an Anthropology of the Good', *Journal of the Royal Anthropological Institute* 19 (3): 447–62.

Roelvink, Gerda, Kevin St Martin and J.K. Gibson-Graham, eds. 2015. *Making Other Worlds Possible: Performing Diverse Economies*. Minneapolis: University of Minnesota Press.

Roitman, Janet. 2014. *Anti-Crisis*. Durham, NC: Duke University Press.

Sanjdorj, M. 1980. *Manchu Chinese Colonial Rule in Northern Mongolia*, translated by Urgunge Onon. London: C. Hurst.

Sassen, Saskia. 2014. *Expulsions: Brutality and Complexity in the Global Economy*. Cambridge, MA: Harvard University Press.

Skafish, Peter and Eduardo Viveiros de Castro. 2016. 'The Metaphysics of Extra-moderns: On the Decolonization of Thought: A Conversation with Eduardo Viveiros de Castro', *Common Knowledge* 22 (3): 393–414.

Sneath, David. 2002. 'Mongolia in the "Age of the Market": Pastoral Land-Use and the Development Discourse'. In *Markets and Moralities: Ethnographies of Postsocialism*, edited by Ruth Mandel and Caroline Humphrey, 191–210. Oxford: Berg.

Sneath, David. 2006. 'Transacting and Enacting: Corruption, Obligation and the Use of Monies in Mongolia', *Ethnos* 71 (1): 89–112.

Sneath, David. 2012. 'The "Age of the Market" and the Regime of Debt: The Role of Credit in the Transformation of Pastoral Mongolia', *Social Anthropology* 20 (4): 458–73.

Spriggs, Hermione, ed. 2018. *Five Heads (Tavan Tolgoi): Art, Anthropology and Mongol Futurism*. Berlin: Sternberg Press.

Stadlen, Alexandra. 2018. 'Weaving Lives from Violence: Possibility and Change for Muslim Women in Rural West Bengal'. PhD thesis, London School of Economic and Political Sciences.

Strathern, Marilyn. 2015. 'Being One, Being Multiple: A Future for Anthropological Relations', *NatureCulture* 3: 122–57.

Thelen, Tatjana. 2011. 'Shortage, Fuzzy Property and Other Dead Ends in the Anthropological Analysis of (Post)Socialism', *Critique of Anthropology* 31 (1): 43–61.

Tsing, Anna. 2005. *Friction: An Ethnography of Global Connection*. Princeton, NJ: Princeton University Press.

Vigh, Henrik. 2008. 'Crisis and Chronicity: Anthropological Perspectives on Continuous Conflict and Decline', *Ethnos* 73 (1): 5–24.

Wagner, Roy. 2018. 'The Reciprocity of Perspectives', *Social Anthropology* 26 (4): 502–10.

Waters, Hedwig A. 2016. 'Living on Loans', *Emerging Subjects Blog*, 22 January. https://blogs.ucl.ac.uk/mongolian-economy/2016/01/22/living-on-loans/.

Waters, Hedwig Amelia. 2018. 'The Financialization of Help: Moneylenders as Economic Translators in the Debt-Based Economy', *Central Asian Survey* 37 (3): 403–18.

Waters, Hedwig Amelia. 2019. '"Living from Loan to Loan": Tracing Networks of Gifts, Debt and Trade in the Mongolian Borderlands'. PhD thesis, University College London.

Yan, Ting. 2017. 'IMF Reaches Staff Level Agreement on the First and Second Reviews of Mongolia's Extended Fund Facility'. Press Release No. 17/411, IMF, 30 October.

Yang, Jie. 2013. '*Song Wennuan*, "Sending Warmth": Unemployment, New Urban Poverty, and the Affective State in China', *Ethnography* 14 (1): 104–25.

Yeung, Ying and Stephen Howes. 2015. 'Resources-to-Cash: A Cautionary Tale from Mongolia'. IM4DC Action Research Report, International Mining for Development Centre.

Zelizer, Viviana A. 2010. *Economic Lives: How Culture Shapes the Economy*. Princeton, NJ: Princeton University Press.

Zigon, Jarrett. 2014. 'An Ethics of Dwelling and a Politics of World-Building: A Critical Response to Ordinary Ethics', *Journal of the Royal Anthropological Institute* 20 (4): 746–64.

Index

Westminster University 59
'white' speech 11, 15
'wild capitalism' 40
'Wolf Economy' 4
women, Mongolian 26

Yang, Jie 87
'yellow heads' 8, 140

zai 14
Zedlen 16, 21, 29–30, 103–15, 148
Zelizer, Viviana A. 45
Zigon, Jarrett 15, 47, 80, 88
Zorig 75–7
zöröö 14

CPSIA information can be obtained
at www.ICGtesting.com
Printed in the USA
BVHW020932121020
590682BV00037B/206